a visual guide to

The

Fortifications
of Malta

Stephen C. Spiteri

photographer
Oliver Gatt

BDL Publishing

© Book Distributors Limited
(+356) 2138 0351
www.bdlbooks.com

Printed in 2017, 2019
This edition, 2022

**A visual guide to the
fortifications of Malta**

Text © Stephen C. Spiteri
Typesetting and design ©
Book Distributors Limited
All photographs © Oliver Gatt

Photo credits:
Xavier Gibert: Fort Binġemma (pp 160,
161) and Fort Delimara (p 173)
Joseph Psaila: Lippija Tower (p 113)
Petar Milošević: Justinian I (p 5)
Tkarpati - St Agatha Tower (cover
photograph)
Nicholas Courtney - Valletta (pp 62-3)

ISBN: 978-99957-67-38-9

CONTENTS

TIMELINE

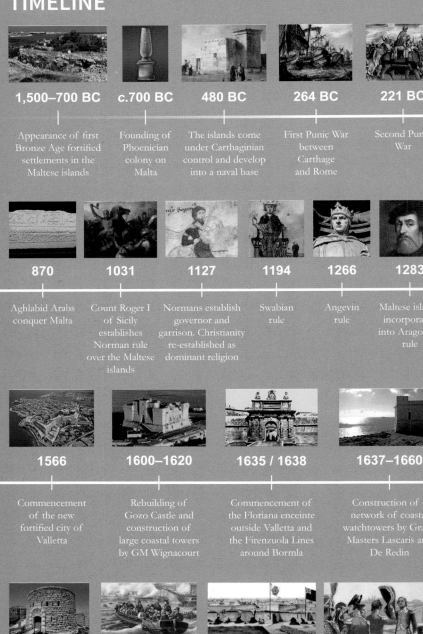

1,500–700 BC

Appearance of first Bronze Age fortified settlements in the Maltese islands

c.700 BC

Founding of Phoenician colony on Malta

480 BC

The islands come under Carthaginian control and develop into a naval base

264 BC

First Punic War between Carthage and Rome

221 BC

Second Punic War

870

Aghlabid Arabs conquer Malta

1031

Count Roger I of Sicily establishes Norman rule over the Maltese islands

1127

Normans establish governor and garrison. Christianity re-established as dominant religion

1194

Swabian rule

1266

Angevin rule

1283

Maltese islands incorporated into Aragonese rule

1566

Commencement of the new fortified city of Valletta

1600–1620

Rebuilding of Gozo Castle and construction of large coastal towers by GM Wignacourt

1635 / 1638

Commencement of the Floriana enceinte outside Valletta and the Firenzuola Lines around Bormla

1637–1660

Construction of a network of coastal watchtowers by Grand Masters Lascaris and De Redin

1793

Building of Fort Tigné

1798

French invasion and the expulsion of the Order of St John from Malta

1798

Maltese rebel against the French and construct batteries around French positions

1800

French Garrison surrenders to Allied Forces after 2-year blockade

TIMELINE

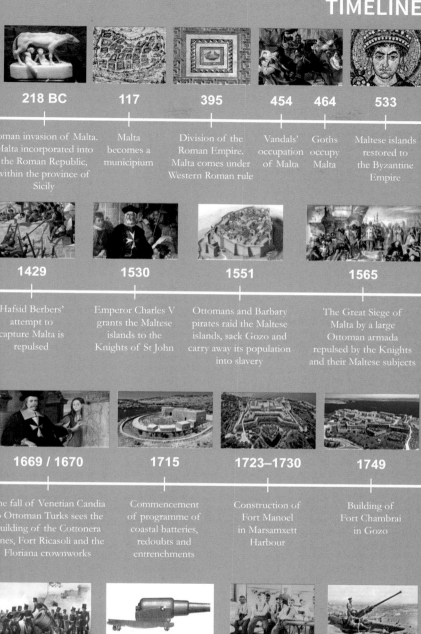

218 BC
Roman invasion of Malta. Malta incorporated into the Roman Republic, within the province of Sicily

117
Malta becomes a municipium

395
Division of the Roman Empire. Malta comes under Western Roman rule

454
Vandals' occupation of Malta

464
Goths occupy Malta

533
Maltese islands restored to the Byzantine Empire

1429
Hafsid Berbers' attempt to capture Malta is repulsed

1530
Emperor Charles V grants the Maltese islands to the Knights of St John

1551
Ottomans and Barbary pirates raid the Maltese islands, sack Gozo and carry away its population into slavery

1565
The Great Siege of Malta by a large Ottoman armada repulsed by the Knights and their Maltese subjects

1669 / 1670
The fall of Venetian Candia to Ottoman Turks sees the building of the Cottonera Lines, Fort Ricasoli and the Floriana crownworks

1715
Commencement of programme of coastal batteries, redoubts and entrenchments

1723–1730
Construction of Fort Manoel in Marsamxett Harbour

1749
Building of Fort Chambrai in Gozo

1814
Malta becomes a British colony

1869–1890
British undertake the re-fortification of Malta with new forts and batteries following the opening of the Suez Canal

1914
Outbreak of WWI

1939
Outbreak of WWII

INTRODUCTION

OVERVIEW

In terms of fortifications, the Maltese islands are unique. Few other islands around the world can boast of such a rich concentration of stone-built defences – in total, some 60 km of ramparts brought together into a small combined surface area that covers little more than 300 km². Surely, few other places can rightfully claim the title of 'island fortress'.

Indeed, no other place around the shores of the Mediterranean can match the diversity of shape and form, as well as the solidity and powerful sculptural features of Malta's ramparts. Together, the fortifications of the Maltese islands make up a rare and unique ensemble of defensive structures – a uniqueness that has long been noted throughout the course of history.

Malta's strategic location in the centre of the Mediterranean Sea.

For the enthusiast of military architecture and fortification in particular, the fortifications of Malta present a rare and easily accessible ensemble of military structures documenting the salient and important developments in the art and science of warfare and fortress-building across an unbroken span of many centuries. Moreover, the variety of design solutions created by the combination of defensive requirements and the nature of the local terrain, coupled with the special qualities of the local building materials and the traditional methods of construction, provide the student of military architecture with a unique opportunity to explore and study this fascinating subject.

This guidebook has been designed to capture and convey this variety of design solutions encountered in the fortifications of Malta and provide a quick visual reference to all the major works.

In many ways, the Maltese islands owe this unique wealth of defensive architecture to its geography. For it was geography that placed Malta in a position of great strategic importance in the centre of the narrow channel joining the eastern and western basins of the Mediterranean, giving it a unique strategic relevance in the history of the region. Secondly, geography also endowed Malta with an excellent natural harbour, one of the finest first-class anchorages to be found anywhere around the shores of the Mediterranean, big enough to accommodate any size of fleet; and thirdly, it furnished the archipelago with an easily worked stone ideal for realizing extensive building programmes.

The first to thoroughly and systematically exploit all these features for military purposes were the Hospitaller Knights of the Order of St John. It was these warrior monks, who first came together in the Holy Land for the protection of pilgrims at the time of the Crusades, who were responsible for starting the process of militarization that was to result in the widespread fortification of the Maltese islands. Prior to the Order's arrival in 1530, Malta and Gozo had been but two of the many small and insecure islands to dot the Mediterranean sea — relatively obscure outposts on the periphery of the Christian world.

Up until the sixteenth century, their only defence had been three puny medieval castles and a few bleak watchtowers. In much earlier epochs, however, both Malta and Gozo had been prosperous enough to each support a substantial walled city and, even earlier, in prehistoric times, the landscape was divided amongst a small number of fortified hilltop villages.

It was, undeniably, the arrival of the Hospitaller Knights of the Order of St John in Malta in 1530 that was to prove the most important turning point in the history of the Maltese islands as far as its fortifications were concerned. For it was these Hospitaller Knights who transformed the islands into a front line military and naval base, an important bulwark of Christendom on the volatile border between the Spanish and Ottoman empires. The larger part of these fortifications was built to the conventions of the bastioned trace and is concentrated around the Grand Harbour area. This was largely because the two-and-a-half centuries of the Order's rule in Malta coincided with the invention, development, and perfection of a style of fortification known as the Italian bastioned system. In all, around

Aerial view of Valletta (centre) and its two harbours: the Grand Harbour (left) and Marsamxett Harbour (right).

25 km of ramparts were erected to provide a defensive apron against a landward investment and a naval bombardment.

The focal point of this complex defensive network was the fortified city of Valletta, the Order's military and political headquarters, begun immediately after the successful resistance to the Ottoman siege of 1565, and which acted as a sort of inner keep in a wide circle of defences. Radiating outwards from it and the enveloping harbour, came, over the course of the seventeenth and eighteenth centuries, an outer network of powerful forts and fortified lines as well as a ring of coastal watch-posts and defensive positions – towers, batteries, redoubts, and entrenchments – designed to warn of approaching enemy vessels and to resist invasion.

This process of fortification came to an abrupt end when the Knights were expelled from Malta in 1798. Ironically, when this much feared attack by a hostile power did finally materialize in 1798, the enemy was not the Ottoman Turk, against whom all that building effort had been directed, but the French under the command of General Napoleon Bonaparte. Indeed, as things turned out, neither the well-thought-out and beautifully engineered design solutions, nor the carefully chosen building materials and time-proven methods employed by the local builders, played any part at all in the drama of the Order's defeat. It was the Order of St John itself, and not the walls with which it had sought to surround itself for centuries, that collapsed from within.

As fate would have it, however, it was not the French but the British who inherited the fabulous prize. Attracted to Malta because of its reputation as a formidable and heavily-fortified station, the British realized that they could not afford to see the Maltese islands fall into the hands of their enemies. So, when the opportunity presented

Napoleon Bonaparte's invasion of Malta in 1798 brought about a sudden end to the Order's 268-year rule.

itself in 1800, they cunningly, and unceremoniously, seized the Maltese islands for themselves. 'I hope we shall never have to give it up,' wrote Lord Nelson after the peace treaty of Amiens was signed in 1802, convinced of Malta's role as an important outer work to India and of its influence 'in the Levant and indeed all the southern parts of Italy'.

For most of the nineteenth century, the British Crown was simply content to occupy the vast network of fortifications which it had inherited from the Knights of St John, without introducing any but minor alterations. It was only around the middle of the nineteenth century that the British military began to voice their concern about the Hospitaller fortifications' ability to withstand the ever increasing destructiveness of a rapidly evolving military technology. Even so, the real British commitment to the fortification of Malta can only be said to have begun to materialize in the late 1860s, following the opening of the Suez Canal in 1869, which gave the island a new strategic role.

By this time, however, both the art of fortress building and the nature of warfare had changed considerably so that the newly-built British defences crystallized into a totally different shape and format from those erected previously by the Hospitaller Knights, forged as they now were from a combination of a new school of military architecture inspired by the polygonal system of Montalambert, imported alien materials such as Portland cement and armour plating, and the acknowledged and proven effectiveness of earthen works against the devastating effects of explosive shells.

The surrender of Malta to the British by the French after a two-year blockade on 4 September 1800.

The British fortifications, however, never acquired the commanding presence and monumentality of the Baroque fortifications built by the Knights, for the forts and fortresses of the industrial age made little provision for aesthetic considerations and visual statements – they were conceived and built as efficient, yet impersonal, killing machines, designed around automated guns and for their most part hidden away from view. Even the limited appeal of the subdued geometric forms of the first modern polygonal forts disappeared altogether once the suppression of outline became the rule. By the end of the 1800s, art no longer had a place in fortress design. What it lacked in aesthetic appeal, however, the modern fort made up for it in technical ingenuity and firepower. The gun, rather than the static walls of the fort itself, became the basis of modern defence.

FORTIFICATIONS IN ANTIQUITY

The story of fortifications in the Maltese islands goes back to prehistoric times. Although archaeological evidence has revealed that the presence of man in Malta dates to around 5000 BC, it was not until the Late Bronze Age that the first fortified settlements began to appear in the islands.

The Late Bronze Age was a period in which turmoil prevailed throughout the whole Mediterranean basin and in those insecure times, the local inhabitants seem to have found refuge on a number of naturally defensible hilltop sites, some of which were strengthened further with man-made walls. Archaeological investigations have located traces of Bronze Age fortified settlements on naturally defensible hilltop sites at Mtarfa, Baħrija, in-Nuffara (Gozo), Ras il-Ġebel (Għajn Tuffieħa), il-Wardija ta' San Ġorġ (Siġġiewi), and Qala Hill (St Paul's Bay) (See Map 2, page 18). Even the ancient capitals of Malta and Gozo themselves appear to stand on sites which originated as prehistoric settlements. In each of these

examples, it was the vertical cliff faces of their hilltop sites which provided the readily available means of protection.

Man-made walls were only used to seal off the most approachable sides of the sites. Toponyms such as Qala, Borġ, and sometimes Wardija, also suggest that areas such as il-Borġ tal-Imramma (also called it-Torri, i.e. the Tower), Ras il-Qala etc., may have been fortified settlements in prehistoric times. Certainly, the most impressive of these early fortified settlements was Borġ in-Nadur (meaning 'fortress on the hill').

This site occupied the seaward tip of a roughly triangular, rocky promontory situated in Marsaxlokk Bay, the most important harbour in the southern part of the island. Although little remains today of the original enceinte, unearthed archaeological remains suggest that this was once an extensive hilltop site defended by thick walls and bastions. The surviving remains reveal a singular D-shaped bastion with adjoining ramparts built of Cyclopean masonry strategically dominating the crest of a small hill.

Opposite and above: Aerial views showing the landward-facing D-shaped bulwark at Borġ in-Nadur Bronze-age settlement (Birżebbuġa) built of Cyclopean masonry. (Map 2 – L14)

PUNIC & ROMAN TIMES

With the coming of the Phoenicians to Malta around 700 BC the island became an important trading station. The Carthaginian colonization, which followed from around the 4th century BC, continued to strengthen this tradition. However, with the increasing rise of the power of Rome, and its ensuing conflict with Carthage, Malta, which lay directly in the zone of conflict between these two great powers, also acquired an important role as a military base. By the time of the first Punic War (262–242 BC), it was serving as a Carthaginian naval base but it was eventually captured by the Romans. It was regained by the Carthaginians who, however, lost it for good in 218 BC in the course of the Second Punic War.

Under the long period of Roman rule the Maltese islands prospered and life was organized around a fortified capital situated in the centre of each island, on the sites now occupied by Mdina and Rabat. The long period of Roman rule introduced a measure of prosperity and this was reflected in the large

and carefully planned fortified towns of Melite and Gaulos. Of the fortifications belonging to this early period, however, very little remains.

The area enclosed within the walls of Roman Melite reached out to what is now the suburb of Rabat. The Maltese historian Ġan Franġisk Abela, writing in the seventeenth century, mentions a perimeter length of about 2 km stiffened with towers and pierced by a number of gates, while its land front is said to have been protected by a wide ditch. In Gozo, the Roman town

Remains of Roman tower situated at Tal-Wilġa, near Luqa airport. (Map 2 – I14)

Agius de Soldanis' drawing of the old Roman city of Melite, present day Mdina. (Map 2 – F11)

occupied the site of the present citadel and its suburb of Rabat.

The Roman defensive effort seems to have also extended to cover other parts of Malta as well. The remains of a series of six so-called 'towers' scattered around the interior of Malta tend to suggest some form of defensive network or a distribution of fortified farms.

Those situated at Tal-Wilġa, Ta' Gawhar, and Ta' Ċieda are amongst the best preserved.

The Roman ramparts of Melite and Gaulos were built with massive hardstone blocks of ashlar, cut down to around 1.5 m in length. The extensive surface quarries still to be found north of Buskett reveal the vast quarrying effort that was necessary to turn out the huge quantities of blocks required to feed the defensive works.

THE MIDDLE AGES

The large-scale organization and building efforts of the Roman period disappeared with the collapse of the Roman empire and in the ensuing dark period of Maltese history. During the

fifth century AD, the Vandals, a Germanic people that ravaged Gaul and Spain, were able to found a kingdom in North Africa, and after establishing a strong navy they began to raid Malta and Sicily. They do not seem to have settled on Malta, and it was the Byzantines who eventually took control of the island in the sixth century AD. The Byzantines held Malta until the year 870, when they were expelled by the Arabs. This Byzantine-Arab period witnessed significant realignments of the walls of the two towns and

Hypothetical reconstruction of the late medieval gateway defences of Mdina showing the barbican, the *Torri Mastra* the and remains of its 'castrum'.

the creation of smaller, more easily defensible, enclosures. In Mdina the process seems to have also been accompanied by the construction of a perimeter fort or castle towards the end of the Byzantine rule. A similar process developed in Gozo whereby the acropolis of the Roman city was converted into a small castle.

The Muslim conquest of Malta in or before 869 AD, according to the Muslim chronicler al-Himyari, was followed by a dismantling of its castle at the hands of Ahmad Ibn Umar, the commander of the Muslim fleet. The stones from this Maltese stronghold, together with that of the Byzantine cathedral, were shipped off to North Africa and used in the construction of the Qasr Habashi of Sousse. A full colonization of the Maltese islands by Muslims, however, seems to have only followed at a much later stage, and the ancient city was once again occupied as the main settlement on the island largely because of its strategic central location. The Muslim defences of Mdina seem to have incorporated much of

the earlier trace of Roman and Byzantine walls, although by this stage the settlement had shrunk to the present-day perimeter.

In 1091 AD the Maltese islands fell to Count Roger the Norman who launched the attack from his kingdom in Sicily.

It is during the Angevin domination that documentary references to Malta become more explicit to enable a broader picture of medieval life on the islands. From thirteenth-century documents we know that a garrison was maintained at Mdina and in the small castle inside the Grand Harbour. Gozo too had its fortress and a garrison.

By the Middle Ages the central fortress in Malta still occupied the site of the old Roman town, although its perimeter had by then been reduced to about a third of its size, its land front defences having been withdrawn back to the present location, an intervention which

Hypothetical reconstruction of the early medieval land front defences of Mdina showing its system of double walls with wall-towers and the castle reinforcing the eastern extremity of the front.

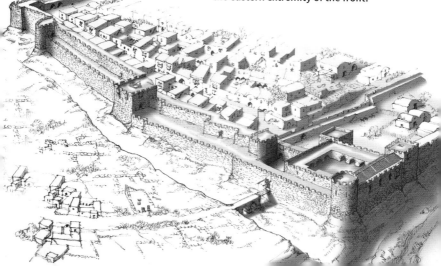

The Castrum Maris (present day Fort St Angelo) in the 1660s – detail from Willem Schellinks' sketch showing the medieval elements of the enceinte and De Guiral's sea-level battery.

many historians attribute to the Byzantines or Arabs. Little survives of the medieval castrum though it is known that it was enclosed by a vertical wall stiffened at intervals by wall-towers, and had at least two gateways on its land front, together with a rock-hewn ditch. The main gate itself appears to have been protected by a turreted barbican by the fifteenth century. Internally, the fortified town was dominated by a castle, but this was dismantled by popular demand around 1453 as it was considered more of a tool for the baronial suppression of the inhabitants rather than for their defence. On the sister island of Gozo the medieval fortress was of much humbler proportions and occupied the site of the present citadel. It is referred to as a castrum by 1241. In 1274, Gozo was sacked by the Genoese, but the castle remained in Sicilian hands.

Undeniably, the most important fortified work in Malta during the Middle Ages was the sea castle situated down in the Grand Harbour – the Castrum Maris (later Fort St Angelo). The history of this fort begins in obscurity, its origins popularly credited to the Arabs who occupied the island in the ninth century AD. However, no mention is made of it in the terms of surrender of the island to Count Roger in 1091. Nor is there any shred of documentary evidence to support the tradition that Count Roger repaired and garrisoned the harbour castle. The first documented evidence to its existence only appears in the 13th century royal mandates during the Angevin domination, where it was referred to as the Castrum Maris. Unlike the inland towns, the sea castle was a purely military establishment, governed by military men in the name of the King and intended to secure the paramountcy of the King's will in local affairs. In 1274 it was garrisoned by 150 loyal and well equipped *servientes gallici boni* under the command of a Castellan.

When the Angevin hold over Malta passed to the Aragonese, the castle and the island were enfeoffed to a succession of feudal lords whose main intent was of exploiting the local resources for their own personal benefit. In 1372, local royalists loyal to Frederick IV recaptured the Castrum Maris from Giacomo Pellegrino of Messina, the royal Captain of Malta who rebelled against the King in an apparent attempt to establish an independent lordship. The 1400s witnessed the growing power of the Hafsids of Tunisia manifesting itself in punishing and destructive raids on Malta and Gozo.

The invention and ever-increasing use of ever-powerful gunpowder-operated artillery in the late fifteenth century rendered the island's medieval strongholds incapable of providing adequate defence against such weapons. The powerful destructive force of cannon called for strong ramparts capable of withstanding the destructive impact of cannon shot. The walls of Mdina, the Castello, and the Castrum Maris, like all medieval strongholds, were only designed to counter scaling and assault. Rebuilding these fortifications to withstand artillery attack required a massive investment which neither the local population nor the Spanish crown

Above: Rear view of Greek's Gate, Mdina. Bottom: Graphic reconstruction showing a general layout of Gozo's medieval castle (today known as Ċittadella) around the time it was taken over by the Hospitaller Knights of St John in 1530.

seem to have been capable or willing to undertake. By the early 1500s, therefore, the Maltese islands' fortifications were not only old and decaying but, worst of all, obsolete.

BRONZE AGE FORTIFIED SITES

1.	Mdina	F11
2.	Ċittadella	K4
3.	In-Nuffara	M4
4.	Ras il-Ġebel	C8
5.	Qala Hill	D7
6.	Wardija	E7
7.	Mosta	G8
8.	Borġ in-Nadur	L14
9.	Wardija ta' San Ġorġ	E14
10.	Il-Qlejgħa	B10

GOZO

Xwejni Bay
Qbajjar Bay
Marsalforn Bay
ŻEBBUĠ
MARSALFORN
Ir-Ramla l-Hamra Bay
San Blas Bay
San Filep Bay
Dahlet Qorrot Bay
XAGĦRA
2
3
KERĊEM
VICTORIA (RABAT)
NADUR
XEWKIJA
QALA
IXAR
GĦAJNSIELEM
TA' SANNAT
MĠARR HARBOUR
Malta Ferry
Hondoq ir-Rummien
St Nicholas Bay
Santa Marija Bay
Mġarr ix-Xini Bay
Ix-Xatt l-Aħmar
Blue Lagoon
Crystal Lagoon

Gozo Ferry
Armier Bay
Paradise Bay
ĊIRKEWWA

St George's Bay
PACEVILLE
St Julian's Bay
TAS-SLIEMA
GŻIRA
MANOEL ISLAND
VALLETTA
TA' XBIEX
TAL-PIETÀ
FLORIANA
ISLA
BIRGU
KALKARA
XGĦAJRA
AMRUN
MARSA
BORMLA
ĦAŻ-ŻABBAR
PAOLA
FGURA
ĦAL TARXIEN
MARSASKALA BAY
SANTA LUĊIJA
ŻEJTUN
MARSASKALA
AL LUQA
HAL GĦAXAQ
St Thomas Bay
GUDJA
8
6
8
MARSAXLOKK
AFI
BIRŻEBBUĠA
St George's Bay
St Peter's Pool
Pretty Bay
Marsaxlokk Bay
Delimara Bay
Kalanka Bay
Malta Freeport
ĦAL FAR

THE HOSPITALLER PERIOD

It was only with the propitious appearance of the Hospitaller Knights on the local scene that new defences *alla moderna* began to materialize. The Hospitaller Knights took possession of the Maltese islands and Tripoli at a time when the technological revolution generated by gunpowder artillery had already conditioned the principles underlying the appearance and development of fortifications. These principles had evolved mainly in Italy and by the mid-sixteenth century there had emerged a consistent style of military architecture which

became known as the Italian style of fortification. This was based on the introduction of the pentagonal bastion.

Still, at first the Hospitallers could not afford to effect but minor modifications to the existing medieval defences. The decision to erect adequate fortifications was then hampered further by the Order's indecision as to whether it ought to settle down in what was seen as a temporary island base. Of the three strongholds, the Hospitallers chose the Castrum Maris and its suburb as their new base – a logical choice dictated by the Rhodian tradition. Being a seafaring body, the Order of St John needed a harbour city from where its naval force could conduct

The Knights of St John, under Grand Master Philippe Villiers de L'Isle-Adam, taking possession of Malta in 1530.

its aggressive maritime activities; the fleet of galleys was the Order's chief instrument of action that perpetuated the fight against the Ottoman Empire in typical crusading tradition. Giacomo Bosio writes that when Grand Master Philippe Villiers de L'Isle-Adam set foot on the island in October 1530, he took up residence in the castle and ordered that Birgu, the suburb of fishermen's and sailors' houses that had grown under the shelter of the castle, be enclosed by a fortified wall. The old castrum itself was fitted out with bastions and cavaliers and renamed Fort St Angelo.

The new works of fortification progressed slowly and it was not until nearly a decade later that Birgu and the old castle were finally enclosed within new bastioned ramparts. The military engineers called in to advise on the new defensive works were quick to point out that the Order had not chosen to fortify the best tactical position inside the Grand Harbour for the ideal site lay instead on the commanding heights of the Sciberras peninsula. The Knights were well aware of this fact – as far back as 1524, a commission of knights sent to evaluate Malta by Grand Master L'Isle-Adam had already realized the great strategic importance of this peninsula, about one mile long and separating the two largest natural harbours on the island.

However desirable this might have been, the Order was then in no position to undertake such an enormous task in the years following its arrival in Malta. The Knights had no other option but to settle down at Birgu and repair as best they could the old castrum. The hope of recapturing Rhodes, too, was still in the hearts of many knights and this continued to fetter the Order's commitment. As a result, no attempt was made to commit the Order's resources to the construction of a large fortified city on what was seen as a temporary island base. Another factor influencing their every decision was the ever-present threat of Turkish retaliatory raids – a state of affairs that made the commencement of any large work of fortification a risky undertaking.

That such fears were not ungrounded was revealed by the Turkish razzia of 1551, which saw an abortive attack by a strong Turkish force and the sacking and devastation of Gozo and its castle, with its population being carried off into slavery. The Turkish armada then set sail for the fortress of Tripoli and this too was captured after a brief siege.

The sacking of Gozo and the attack on Birgu and Mdina served to reveal the weakness of the Order's position and left no doubt at all as to the gravity of the Turkish threat. The Hospitallers reacted by stiffening the island's defences as best they could. Immediately, work began on the construction of a small fort (named St Elmo) at the tip of Sciberras peninsula while a second one, Fort St Michael, was erected on the Isola peninsula adjoining Birgu. So acute was the sense of urgency induced by the fear of a renewed Turkish attack that the Order had both forts practically ready by March 1552. During the brief reign of Grand Master Claude de la Sengle, Fort St Michael was enclosed within a bastioned enceinte and a new town, Senglea, sprang up within its walls.

Hospitaller Knights and the building of fortifications.

It was the election of Jean de Valette to the magistracy which saw renewed enthusiasm for a new fortress on Sciberras heights. In 1558, Bartolomeo Genga, one of the foremost European military engineers, was persuaded to visit Malta to draw up the plans for the new city. Genga, however, died in Malta before work could begin on the fortress he had designed. The deterioration in the general military situation brought about by the Djerba crisis induced the Knights to attempt to entrench themselves more securely on the island, with the Order's first reaction being to petition for the services of another good engineer from the grand duke of Florence – a demand that resulted in the loan of Baldassere Lanci. This Italian engineer was brought over in 1562 to design the new fortress, and by the following year the project had received papal approval but once again the Order did not press on with the building of the fortress. It appears that by 1563 the menace of a Turkish reprisal had become more apparent, and the Knights probably felt sure that a major attack was imminent.

This finally materialized in May 1565. The Turks were quick to exploit the basic weakness that threatened all the Knights' defensive positions: the high ground that overlooked them. Turkish engineers made good use of this land feature by setting up powerful batteries with which they hammered and softened the walls in preparation for major infantry assaults. The first to fall to the enemy was Fort St Elmo, after a month-long siege. The Turks then turned their attention to the fortresses of Birgu and Senglea. As the siege dragged on, Turkish strength and morale declined rapidly, but still it was the arrival of a large Christian relief force in early September that finally convinced the Turks to abandon their enterprise and set sail back to Constantinople.

The successful conclusion of the siege, whilst a matter of great rejoicing among the princes of Europe, had weakened the Order considerably. All the forts were ruined, huge debts had been incurred, and many knights had been killed in battle. Through the financial and military support of the European monarchs and the Pope, the Order set about building a new fortified city on Sciberras heights. Pope Pius IV himself, anxious that the Order remained in Malta, offered immediate financial assistance and sent over one of his best military engineers, Francesco Laparelli, to design the new fortress. Laparelli arrived in Malta in December 1565 and promptly set about preparing the plans for the new city. This he established on the highest part of the peninsula, with its four-bastioned land front some 500 metres from St Elmo. The enceinte was to be strengthened further with nine cavaliers, of which only two, however, were actually built.

The first stone was laid by Grand Master Jean de Valette on 28 March 1566 and work progressed rapidly. The new city within the Valletta fortifications was built to a grid pattern with a systematic distribution and division of streets. That part of Laparelli's design which was not executed was the construction of an arsenal and the Manderaggio, or galley pen. Laparelli left Malta in 1569 and entrusted the continuation of the work to Gerolamo Cassar. He volunteered for service with the Papal fleet and died of the plague at Candia in the following year.

The lifting of the siege. The outnumbered defenders had managed to withstand a siege of more than four months despite the numerical superiority of the Ottoman forces stacked against them.

The harbour fortifications in the late seventeenth century. In the centre is Valletta with its powerful outworks in the form of Pietro Paolo Floriani's enceinte and Valperga's faussebraye and crowned hornworks.

By 1571 the Valletta fortifications had reached an advanced stage in their construction and the Order felt safe enough to transfer its convent there from Birgu. The building of the fortified city of Valletta heralded an important phase in the development of the harbour fortifications. This decision was to spark off a chain reaction of fortress-building that was to occupy the Order for the rest of its stay on the island.

THE SEVENTEENTH CENTURY

By the early years of the seventeenth century various engineers and military experts had realized that, although Valletta was well designed, its land front lacked strong outworks – devices that were then becoming increasingly essential in keeping enemy siege batteries as far as possible from the main walls.

As a result, in 1635, a new enceinte was designed by the Italian engineer Pietro Paolo Floriani and built ahead of the old Valletta front. The new works, known as the Floriana Lines, however, came in for much criticism from the start, mainly because these were considered to be enormous and required too much money to build and too many men to garrison. Nonetheless, work on these fortifications went ahead, but the moment Floriani returned to Italy, the Knights began to doubt the merits of the whole scheme.

Serious complications really began to arise when a new project, the Sta Margherita Lines, designed by Vincenzo Maculano da Firenzuola to enclose the Birgu and Senglea fronts, was initiated in 1638. After the Great Siege, the towns of Birgu and Senglea, renamed Città Vittoriosa and Città Invicta respectively, were repaired but thereafter little was done to improve their defences for, commanded as they were by the surrounding high ground, they remained badly situated in a pit-like amphitheatre. The Sta Margherita Lines were thus intended to secure these heights and remove once and for all the threat posed to the two fortresses, but the money soon ran out.

Work on both the Floriana and Sta Margherita Lines dragged on interminably and neither scheme was completed before well into the 1700s, by which time both works had been subjected to a number of improvements. In the 1670s the Floriana front was fitted with a faussebraye and a crowned hornwork designed by the Italian engineer Antonio Maurizio Valperga, while the Sta Margherita Lines were enclosed within a far more ambitious ring of fortifications known as the Cottonera Lines, also designed by Valperga.

The Cottonera Lines, named after Grand Master Nicholas Cotoner, who commissioned their construction, were effectively the most ambitious work of fortification ever undertaken by the Knights of St John in Malta. Built as a result of the fall of Candia to the Turks in 1669 and the rekindled fear of a Turkish invasion, these consisted of a massive trace of eight large bastions, encircling the Sta Margherita and San Salvatore hills and joining the extremities of the old fronts of Vittoriosa and Senglea. Work on the Cottonera Lines began in August 1670 and continued incessantly for a decade until the death of the grand master in 1680, by which time the main body of the enceinte had already been laid down under the supervision of Mederico Blondel, the Order's resident engineer. The funds allocated for the Cottonera fortifications had run out and the new grand master ordered the cessation of the project. As a result the ravelins and cavaliers, together with the ditch and the

Painting showing the harbour fortifications in the second half of the eighteenth century. In the foreground are Senglea (left) and Fort St Angelo (right). Valletta and Floriana are in the middle and in the distance is Fort Manoel commanding Marsamxett Harbour.

covertway that were originally proposed by Valperga, were never constructed. The project remained virtually abandoned until well into the eighteenth century, when some effort was made to bring the works to completion. Valperga also designed and built Fort Ricasoli, which was erected to secure the harbour entrance.

THE EIGHTEENTH CENTURY

The 1700s mark the last phase of the Order's fortification of the Maltese islands, witnessing the refortification of the old capitals of Malta and Gozo, and these two citadels owe their present shape to the works undertaken during this period.

An important element of the island's defences introduced during the seventeenth century were the coastal fortifications. Between 1605 and 1620, massive towers sprung up at Mġarr (Gozo), St Paul's Bay, Marsaxlokk, St Thomas Bay, Marsalforn (Gozo), Comino and Sta Maria delle Grazie at the expense of Grand Master Alof de Wignacourt. Other smaller watchtowers spread out within visual distance of each other soon followed these large towers. Six were built by Grand Master Lascaris between 1636 and 1657, together with another large tower at Mellieħa. These were augmented by a further thirteen towers built by Grand Master Martin de Redin in Malta.

After 1660 the enthusiasm for coastal defences appears to have waned, and it was only at the start of the eighteenth century that the Order once again began to show a renewed interest in coastal defence. Under the influence of French military engineers, a network of coastal defences was implemented, which incorporated gun batteries, redoubts, entrenchments, and later, fougasses.

The strategy was aimed to secure all the bays so as to prevent an enemy

Above: Grand Master Cottoner and his fortified lines.
Left: The fortified towns of Birgu and Senglea in the 1600s.

from disembarking troops and, in trying to do so, suffer heavy losses and be unable to mount a siege of the main harbour positions.

The eighteenth century saw the Order also preoccupied with the fortification of Marsamxett Harbour in an attempt to secure the vulnerable western side of Valletta, which was still devoid of any fortification whatsoever. The greatest threat posed to Valletta was from the Isoletto, a small leaf-shaped island on which was located the quarantine hospital, and there in 1723 the Knights began to construct a star-shaped fort based on the design of French military engineers. The design of Fort Manoel (so-called in honour of Grand Master Vilhena, who financed the work) was prepared by the French military engineer Charles François de Mondion. Its low silhouette and system of bastioned trace, making the widest use of crossfire to sweep the approaches, was then in line with the latest developments in the art of fortification.

With the Isoletto secured, the Knights then turned their

Above: Detail from a painting in the National Museum of Fine Arts showing various coastal towers and batteries along part of the island's shores.
Below: Fort Manoel and Marsamxett Harbour with the fortified city of Valletta in the background.

attention to Dragut Point at the mouth of Marsamxett, but it was not until 1793, however, that the Order could afford to undertake the construction of

a fort there. Fort Tigné, as the new fort designed by the military engineer Antoine Etienne de Tousard was called, however, was a very small work by eighteenth-century standards, actually more of a large redoubt than a veritable fort, but its design was probably the most revolutionary of all the fortifications built by the Knights. In plan, it consisted of a diamond-shaped casemated work with a strong circular bomb-proof keep occupying the rear salient. It was surrounded by a ditch and an elaborate system of countermines. Its most important features were the three counterscarp musketry galleries. The design of Fort Tigné was heavily influenced by the writings of Montalembert and more particularly by the lunettes built by the French general Jean-Claude Lemichaud d'Arcon. By the end of the eighteenth century, the supremacy of the bastioned system was being challenged by the growing popularity of the tenaille trace. The new style of fortification known as the polygonal system, of which Fort Tigné is one of the earliest examples, was to dominate the science of military architecture through most of the following century.

Early eighteenth-century etching showing the harbour defences of Marsamxett Harbour with what appears to be Fort Manoel's guns firing. Fort St Elmo protects the entrance to the harbours while the Floriana enceinte protects the landward approaches to the Valletta's land front. In the background, the Grand Harbour is punctuated by Fort Ricasoli, Fort St Angelo and Birgu, and Senglea.

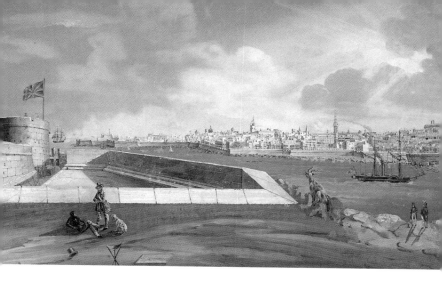

THE FRENCH INTERLUDE

Fort Tigné marks the last of the fortifications built by the Knights in Malta. For more than two centuries, the defence of the Maltese islands had been the Order's primary concern, to which it devoted a large part of its resources. The enemy was always seen to be the Turk, yet when the attack by a hostile power finally materialized in 1798, it was not the Turks but the French under the command of General Napoleon Bonaparte. As things turned out, the fortifications were never put to the test; the network of coastal fortifications was outflanked and the system of opposing the enemy in the countryside discredited while the major fortresses capitulated with hardly a shot being fired. The premature surrender of the fortifications, on the first occasion on which they were put to the test, cannot be blamed on their design or condition. The Order had collapsed from within.

The French capture of Malta was no accidental affair. In April of 1798 the Executive Directory instructed Napoleon to seize the island of Malta, but only if this

Above: Fort Tigné from a watercolour by Louis Taffien 1811–1866 with Valletta and Fort St Elmo in the distance.
Below: German Grand Master Ferdinand von Hompesch, the last Grand Master to rule over Malta.

could be accomplished without compromising the success of the Orient expedition. The fall of Malta, however, was inevitable, for by the end of the 18th century, the Order of St John, impoverished and anachronistic, and ruling over an alienated population, had reached its lowest ebb. Napoleon's troops, aided by a strong fifth columnist party involving many of the senior Hospitaller Knights themselves, seized the islands with hardly a shot being fired.

The inhabitants' initial reception of the Republican occupation, however, was rapidly replaced by a disillusionment which, in the space of a mere three months, erupted into open rebellion. The French reacted by barricading themselves inside the safety of the formidable harbour fortifications. The struggle quickly evolved into a stalemate with the Maltese in control of the countryside and the French firmly in command of the fortified harbour enclave.

The French force, under the able command of General Vaubois, consisting of 3,053 infantry and five companies of artillery, was well armed and well led. The Maltese insurgents, on the other hand, numbered around 10,000 men, of which only 2,358 were adequately armed. The two sides sat and faced each other, the French behind the safety of the formidable harbour fortifications and the Maltese from behind their positions, which enveloped the harbour defences within a large semicircular contravallation of field walls stiffened at strategic intervals by camps and batteries, spanning all the way from in front of Fort Tigné right round to St Rocco, opposite Fort Ricasoli. The insurgents' main camps were situated at Ħal Għargħur, San Giuseppe, Tas-Samra, Corradino, Ħal Tarxien, Żejtun and Ħaż-Żabbar, and each was responsible for a number of gun batteries spread out in the neighbouring countryside.

The French, on their part, were content to simply hold out until the arrival of reinforcements, but the Maltese were desperate and sought foreign assistance. A number of delegates were dispatched to Sicily to implore the help of the King of the Two Sicilies, and somewhere off the coast of Sicily they were intercepted by the British fleet under the command of Lord Nelson, then returning from its victory at the Battle of the Nile. Soon, British and Portuguese ships were standing outside the mouth of the Grand Harbour, effecting a blockade of the French, and allied troops were landed to assist the Maltese insurgents in their struggle.

Napoleon Bonaparte.

Tal-Borġ Battery and Camp (Ħal Tarxien) set up by the Maltese insurgents in 1798 to control the French garrison in Cottonera.

After two years of blockade, with their stocks of food practically exhausted and convinced that there was no hope of receiving any help or reinforcements, the French force in Malta capitulated to the British on 4 September 1800. The following day, British soldiers entered the fortifications of Floriana, Tigné and Ricasoli and hoisted the Union Jack over the harbour fortifications. The situation following the French departure from Malta, however, remained undecided and when the peace treaty of Amiens was signed in May 1802, Great Britain made certain commitments to evacuate its forces from Malta, while the island itself was to be restored to the Order of St John of Jerusalem under the protection and guarantee of a third power – Russia. The short period of peace that followed the treaty ended before this clause could be fulfilled. When hostilities recommenced in May 1803, the British forces were still stationed on the island, and with the Treaty of Paris, Malta was recognized as belonging in full right and sovereignty to Britain.

A contemporary drawing showing a sortie by the besieged French garrison from the Cottonera fortifications against the Maltese insurgents' front line positions at Corradino, 1798.

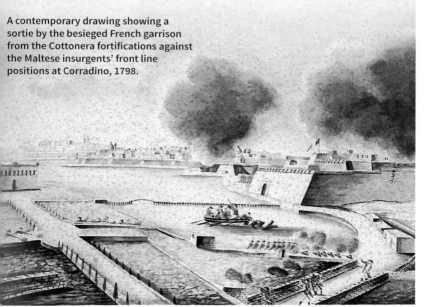

A BRITISH COLONY

On gaining possession of Malta the British found themselves occupying one of the most formidable fortresses in the Mediterranean. By the end of the eighteenth century, following more than two hundred years of continual building activity, the Hospitaller Knights had created a vast network of permanent stone fortifications, most of which were mainly concentrated around the two deep water anchorages of the Grand Harbour and Marsamxett. The whole harbour area, indeed the whole island with its coastal towers, batteries and entrenchments, had been transformed into one large fortress with the city of Valletta as its inner keep.

Throughout most of the first half of the nineteenth century the British military did not attempt to create any additional work of fortification. The main concern was the harbour fortifications and

although the network of coastal defences was initially retained in service, the towers, batteries, and entrenchments were gradually abandoned by the 1830s.

There were two main reasons for this state of affairs. To begin with, there had been no significant development in the science of warfare during this period to render obsolete the vast apron of seventeenth- and eighteenth-century bastions built by the Knights. Secondly, it would have required a considerably large invading force to subdue these defences, and with the Royal Navy's powerful Mediterranean fleet based at Malta there was very little chance that such an armada could hope to reach the island without first

British troops on exercise along the Victoria Lines in the area of ix-Xagħra ta' Binġemma.

A coastal muzzle-loading gun on traversing sliding carriage in a casemated emplacement.

running the gauntlet of the British ships – the defence of Malta rested primarily on the shoulders of the British navy, and at sea Britannia ruled the waves.

It was the opening of the Suez Canal in 1869, more than anything else, that was to prove instrumental in enhancing Malta's strategic role in the Mediterranean, particularly as a staging-post on the Levant route to India and Asia and, consequently, in refocusing Britain's attention onto the urgent need for new defences. The 1870s, as a result, saw the main British effort in the fortification of Malta. Initially the works undertaken comprised mainly the reconstruction of the old harbour defences to take the new heavy armament, but this soon spread to cover most of the coastline with new coastal forts and batteries. The land defences too were given attention and a new front was established along a ridge of commanding ground north of Mdina. This new extended perimeter retained the resources of the greater part of the country on the side of the defenders.

Work on what was originally to be called the North-West Front began in 1875 and comprised a string of isolated forts and batteries – Forts Binġemma and Madalena controlled the western and eastern extremities respectively, while Fort Mosta and a strong defensive perimeter known as the Dwejra Lines (1881) commanded the centre. Various small batteries were also added to fill in weak gaps in the front. These defensive works were eventually linked together by a continuous infantry line and the whole front was renamed the Victoria Lines in 1897 in order to commemorate the Diamond Jubilee of Queen Victoria.

Work on the coastal forts, all built in the polygonal style, progressed quite rapidly, and by 1878 five forts had been completed, namely Sliema,

St Rocco, Pembroke, St Lucian, and Tas-Silġ, while two other major forts, Delimara and San Leonardo, were fast nearing completion. The most important feature of these new British Forts was their armament – a new generation of large, rifled-muzzle loaders (RML) capable of firing heavy shells. These Victorian fortifications consisted basically of three types – forts, coastal batteries and defensive lines. In all, some 11 forts, 12 batteries, and 3 sets of fortified lines were erected to protect the island. Gozo was not included in the defensive scheme and remained unfortified.

During the twentieth century, the 'fortress' strategy of defence was no longer considered to be effective and was abandoned in favour of a policy that required that the island's defence be conducted from its shores. The Victoria Lines were discarded as an inland front line

British gunners loading a heavy anti-aircraft gun.

of defence, and the new century witnessed a deliberate effort devoted to the spreading out of the defensive structures over most of the rest of the island.

The years leading up to the First World War were also accompanied by a radical standardization of the armament of coastal fortifications. A number of coastal forts and batteries were, as a result, de-activated as the defences were reviewed. By 1914 the coastal defences of Malta were armed with sixteen 9.2-inch guns, twenty 6-inch guns and fourteen 12-pdr QF guns, manned by eight companies of the Royal Garrison Artillery and three companies of the Royal Malta Artillery. Some ten forts and batteries were struck off the list of works of fortifications considered necessary for the mounting of approved armaments.

During the Great War in Europe in 1914, the defence of Malta as a naval base was not a priority, and

A Bofors anti-aircraft gun in its protective sangar at the Upper Barrakka garden in WWII.

throughout the war, only one new battery (Wolseley) was erected. By the outbreak of the Second World War in 1939, the coastal defences had once again been re-organized and re-deployed, the total number of guns being nearly halved in the process, as another five forts and batteries had been closed down. The 1930s, however, saw the introduction of a new type of fortification – concrete pillboxes and anti-aircraft batteries. The pillboxes were mainly machine gun emplacements protected with concrete walls. These mushroomed with the outbreak of hostilities in 1939 into a series of stop lines and nodal strong points around beaches, airfields and other installations. Vast stretches of accessible coastline were planted with barbed wire entanglements, mined and defended with field guns. As things turned out it was mainly the anti-aircraft batteries which took the brunt of Malta's defence. In 1942, heavy anti-aircraft defences comprised a total of 112 guns deployed in 29 troop positions of four guns each, and 2 of two guns each. The heavy anti-aircraft guns (HAA) were deployed roughly in three concentric circles, the inner one of which enveloped the harbour area and the other two the aerodromes and military installations. Added to these were 40-mm Bofors light anti-aircraft guns deployed around airfields and harbours.

After the War, there was one final major re-armament programme involving two batteries of 5.25-inch dual purpose guns (Coast and Anti-Aircraft) installed at Fort Benghisa and Fort St Rocco in 1950. By 1960, however, all the fortifications were closed down and disarmed bringing to an end the active role of fortifications in the defence of the island.

Long bands of coastal barbed wire entanglements were the island's first front line of defence against a seaborne invasion during the Second World War.

HOSPITALLER FORTIFICATIONS

FORTS

1

MDINA

MDINA – CITTÀ NOTABILE, CITTÀ VECCHIA

Map 1 – F11

Medieval, 1540–1560, 1650, 1720s, 1739

Mdina (Città Notabile or Città Vecchia) was the ancient capital of Malta before the arrival of the Knights in 1530. Its landlocked position in the centre of the island and obsolete medieval walls meant that it held very little military advantage for the Knights, who preferred to settle down inside the harbour close to their fleet of galleys. Little resources were expanded on the improvement of its defences, and the town survived the Turkish invasion of 1565 largely because the Turks chose to ignore it. The building of the new city of Valletta then helped to contribute towards the decline of the old town so that by the mid-seventeenth century Mdina was in a very bad state of repair. A new lease of life was given to Mdina during the reign of Grand Master Martin de Redin, who undertook the repairs to its ramparts and initiated the construction of new fortifications, including a large central bastion on the land front. The death of this grand master in 1660 brought the town's rehabilitation to an abrupt halt while the earthquake of 1693 severely damaged many buildings inside the walls.

A true revival of the old city really came with the arrival of French military engineers in the early eighteenth century, particularly during the reign of Grand Master Manoel de Vilhena, and Mdina owes its final form, its palaces, fortifications, and Baroque buildings and gateways, to the works undertaken during this period of its history. The works were undertaken by the Order's military engineer Charles François de Mondion. The last addition to the defences, a bastion erected to the rear of the cathedral, was made in 1739.

General layout of Mdina's fortifications as these would have stood around 1798

1. D'Homedes (St Paul) Bastion (16th c.)
2. Land front ditch
3. Old medieval gate (walled up)
4. Main Baroque gateway (18th c.)
5. *Torre dello Standardo*
6. De Redin Bastion (mid-17th c.)
7. Covertway (no longer existent)
8. Greeks' Gate (Baroque period – original medieval gate is set inside it and opens into the city)
9. St Peter Bastion (16th c.)
10. Magazine Curtain (casemated)
11. St Mary (Ta' Bachar) Bastion (16th c.)
12. Medieval wall-tower
13. Despuig Bastion (1739)
14. Old enceinte with medieval remains and early Hospitaller walls
15. Battery of faussebraye with sally port
16. Bastionette (18th c.)
17. Scarp musketry gallery (18th c.)

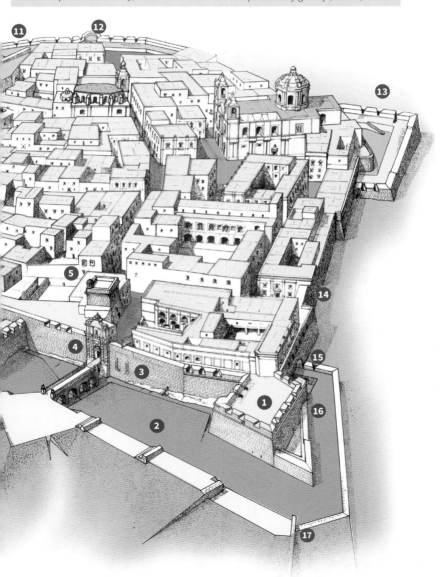

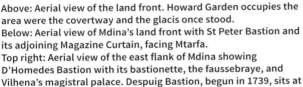

Above: Aerial view of the land front. Howard Garden occupies the area were the covertway and the glacis once stood.

Below: Aerial view of Mdina's land front with St Peter Bastion and its adjoining Magazine Curtain, facing Mtarfa.

Top right: Aerial view of the east flank of Mdina showing D'Homedes Bastion with its bastionette, the faussebraye, and Vilhena's magistral palace. Despuig Bastion, begun in 1739, sits at the foot of the ramparts to the rear of the Cathedral.

Middle right: Mdina's Baroque main gate.

Bottom right: Sally port in the flank of D'Homedes Bastion.

View of Mdina's northern enceinte showing the medieval wall-tower, St Mary Bastion, Magazine Curtain, and St Peter Bastion.

2 CITTADELLA

VICTORIA (RABAT), GOZO

Map 1 – K4

Medieval, 1599–1622

By the time of the Order's arrival in Malta in 1530, the oldest standing work of fortification on the island of Gozo was the Gran Castello, or Cittadella, as it later came to be known. This was a small landlocked stronghold which at best served as a refuge for the local population in times of danger. Even so, in 1551, the Turks under Sinan Pasha encountered little difficulty in

reducing it to ruins in the course of a devastating *razzia* in which some 6,000 Gozitans found sheltering therein were carried off into slavery.

Although the castle was rebuilt, Gozo remained practically uninhabited for many decades after. In a bid to attract settlers to the island by providing some measure of security through the building of a powerful fortress, attempts were made in 1599 to seek a permanent solution for the defence of Gozo. To this end the Order secured the services of Giovanni Rinaldini, an Anconitan engineer, and the

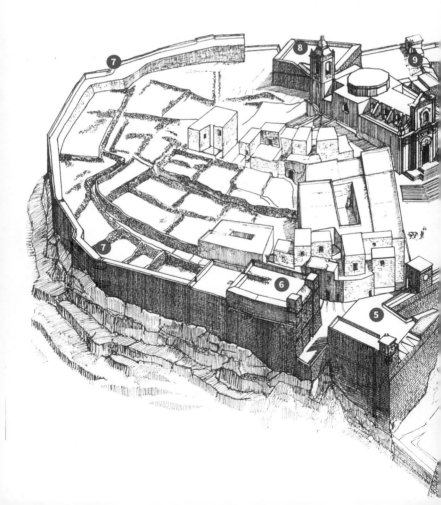

View of the bastioned enceinte showing St John Demi-bastion and its commanding cavalier, the low battery, and part of the medieval enceinte.

old castle was practically rebuilt and fitted out with bastions and cavaliers, a ditch with covertway and glacis and a ravelin protecting the entrance into the citadel, all of which served to give it its present form. Although the bastioned ramparts gave the old fortress a new lease of life, its landlocked position remained a serious problem, and as such the Knights could not derive much military advantage from the newly-rebuilt stronghold. Eventually, a new fortress was built closer to the sea, at Mġarr (Fort Chambrai), but even so the old citadel was never actually abandoned and remained the seat of the local government until its surrender to the French invading forces in the summer of 1798.

General layout of the Cittadella's fortifications as these would have stood around 1798

1. Ravelin with advance gate
2. Land-front ditch
3. St Michael Bastion
4. Main gateway
5. St Martin Demi-bastion
6. St Martin Cavalier
7. Medieval ramparts with chemin de ronde
8. St John Cavalier
9. St John Demi-bastion
10. Covertway with place-of-arms

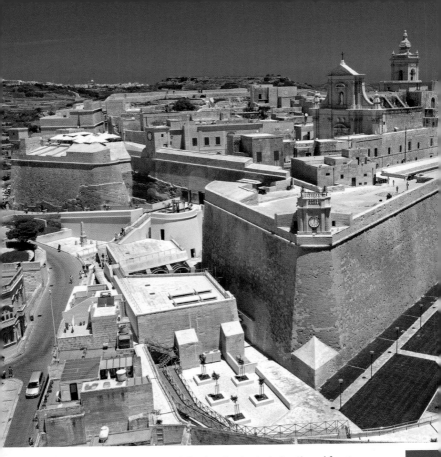

Above: Aerial view of the Cittadella showing its main bastioned front.
Below: Aerial view of the Cittadella showing its northern medieval enceinte and cliff face.
Top right: Detail of St John Demi-bastion, cavalier and battery.
Centre right: View of the main land front.
Bottom right: Aerial view of the northeastern part of the enceinte showing St John Demi-bastion and the small battery grafted at the foot of the medieval walls built to close off the ditch.

3 FORT ST ANGELO
BIRGU (VITTORIOSA)

Map 1 – L10

Medieval, 1540s, 1680s

Fort St Angelo is the oldest fort in the harbour area. The first documented evidence to its existence appears in thirteenth-century royal mandates during the Angevin domination (1266–1284) of Malta, where it was referred to as the Castrum Maris. As the only existing fortification in the Grand Harbour, it was taken over by the Knights on their coming to Malta in 1530 and established as their headquarters. The first significant alterations were the excavation of a moat to isolate it from the mainland and the construction of a narrow bastioned front with a singular

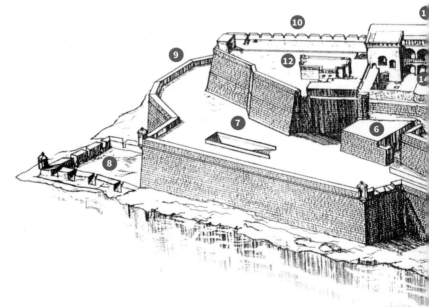

General layout of Fort St Angelo's fortifications as these would have stood around 1798

1. D'Homedes Bastion
2. Sea-filled moat
3. Main gate
4. Ferramolino's Cavalier
5. Barbican
6. Gunpowder magazine
7. Ramp leading down to sally port
8. De Guiral Battery
9. Grunenburg's enceinte
10. Grunenburg's uppermost battery
11. Magistral palace (old keep of original castle)
12. Chapel of St Anne
13. Barracks
14. Remains of medieval tower of inner bailey
15. Inner gate behind barbican

bastion and cavalier, the latter designed by the Italian military engineer Antonio Ferramolino. During the Great Siege of 1565, Fort St Angelo served as the keep of the Order's defensive position. The next major alterations to Fort St Angelo were undertaken in the 1680s when Colonel Don Carlos de Grunenburg, engineer to the Viceroy of Sicily, proposed and financed the rebuilding of the castle to incorporate four tiers of batteries facing the mouth of the harbour. These works gave the fort its present day appearance.

Main gate of Fort St Angelo following its restoration by Heritage Malta.

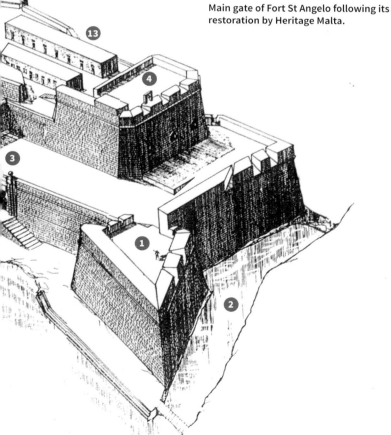

Above: Aerial view of Fort St Angelo.

Left: Aerial view of Fort St Angelo showing the four tiers of batteries designed by Carlos de Grunenburg and built in the last decade of the seventeenth century.

Right, from top to bottom: The church of St Anne as partly rebuilt in the 19th century; Interior of the church of St Anne with its Hospitaller and medieval elements; One of the domed echaugettes (sentry boxes) which guarded the perimeter of the fort; View of the magistral palace inside the *inner castrum* area of the fort, originally the Castellan's residence.

4 BIRGU

BIRGU – CITTÀ VITTORIOSA

Map 1 – L10, L11
Medieval, 1530s–1565, 1720s

The Hospitallers' first major work of fortification after they had settled down on the island in 1530 was to enclose the town of Birgu within a fortified enceinte and thereby convert it into the first of a series of bastioned fortified cities within the Grand Harbour area.

Although works on the new fortress progressed slowly, by the time of the Great Siege in 1565, the stronghold of Birgu had been built up into a powerful bastioned enceinte protected by strong bastions, a cavalier and a deep ditch. Its defences, although breached in a number of places, managed to withstand repeated artillery bombardment and infantry assaults

during the course of the Turkish siege, earning it the title of *Città Vittoriosa* (the Victorious City). Although respecting the footprint of much of the original layout, the present fortifications and ramparts are largely the product of a vast refortification project undertaken during the early decades of the eighteenth century under the direction of the French military engineer, Mondion.

These works involved, amongst many other things, the construction of the bastioned retrenchment at the Post of Castile, the rebuilding of the two land front bastions and the introduction of a bent entrance approach into the town through a system of three gateways. The British effected no structural alterations to the Birgu defences, limiting their interventions mainly to the reconstruction of embrasures and gun platforms to take traversing gun carriages and larger calibre SB (smooth-bore) guns.

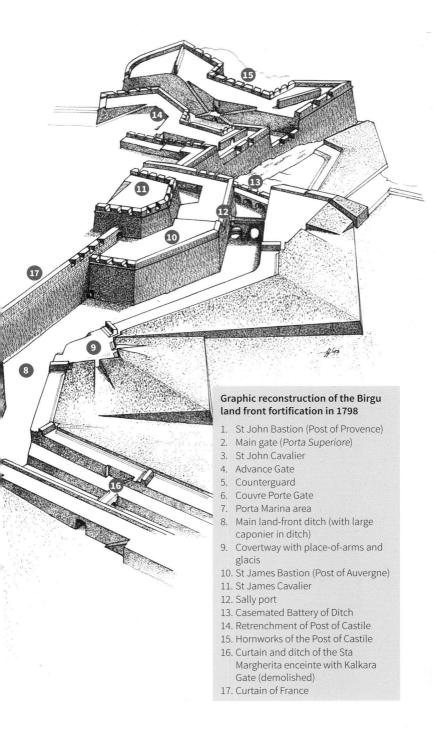

Graphic reconstruction of the Birgu land front fortification in 1798

1. St John Bastion (Post of Provence)
2. Main gate (*Porta Superiore*)
3. St John Cavalier
4. Advance Gate
5. Counterguard
6. Couvre Porte Gate
7. Porta Marina area
8. Main land-front ditch (with large caponier in ditch)
9. Covertway with place-of-arms and glacis
10. St James Bastion (Post of Auvergne)
11. St James Cavalier
12. Sally port
13. Casemated Battery of Ditch
14. Retrenchment of Post of Castile
15. Hornworks of the Post of Castile
16. Curtain and ditch of the Sta Margherita enceinte with Kalkara Gate (demolished)
17. Curtain of France

Left: The main Baroque gateways into the fortified city of Birgu:

Top: Couvre Porte gate.
Centre: Porta Superiore (main gate).
Bottom: Sally port with bridge in left face of St James Bastion.

Above: View of the right face of St John Bastion with the Advance Gate and the bridge leading to it which connects with the gorge of the counterguard.
Right: Parapet with embrasures on the terrace of the casemated battery in the flank of St John Bastion (Post of Provence).

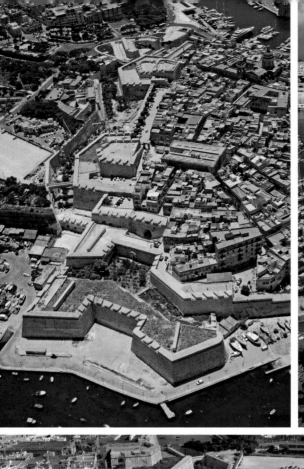

Various aerial views of the fortifications of Birgu:
Top left: The hornwork of the Post of Castile.
Top right: Birgu's land front showing the two bastions with cavaliers and ditch.
Right: Ditch and gorge of the retrenchment of the hornwork of the Post of Castile.
Left: The Counterguard (Couvre Porte) and entrance way into the fortified town via its three gates.

5 FORT ST ELMO
VALLETTA

Map 1 – L10

1552, 1680s/ 1720s/ 19th c./20th c.

Fort St Elmo was built in 1552 as a direct reaction to the Turkish corsair *razzia* of the previous year. It was designed to control the entrances to both the Grand Harbour and that of Marsamxett. So acute was the sense of urgency that the fort was built and completed in less than six months. This excessive haste, however, soon began to manifest itself in a number of serious defects inherent both in the design of the fort and in the choice of its location. Consequently, considerable effort had to be reinvested to remedy these faults, which by 1565 had actually involved the addition of a large detached triangular cavalier, a ravelin, and a few other hastily built

View of the echaugette on the salient of the left demi-bastion with British period musketry parapet.

outworks. During the Great Siege of 1565, Fort St Elmo received the initial brunt of the Turkish attack, and it was its stubborn and lengthy resistance that proved to be the turning point of the Turkish defeat. In the aftermath of the siege, Fort St Elmo was quickly rebuilt. With the foundation of the new

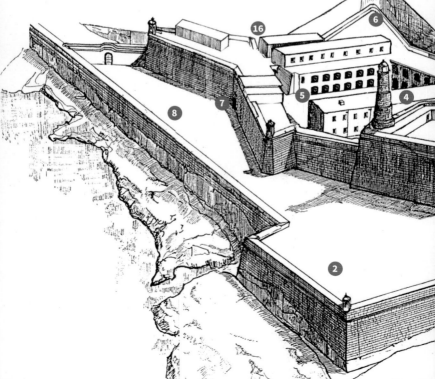

enceinte of Valletta, particularly after the fort was enclosed with a vast apron of bastions – known as the Carafa enceinte built during the 1680s – its role was eventually changed to that of a keep of the new fortress.

The British, in 1800, immediately realized the importance of this fort to the security of the harbour and continued to invest in its defences, upgrading both its armament and its resistance to bombardment. The sea-front defences received considerable attention. It was the outer ring of bastions, and the cavalier, which housed a succession of heavy RML guns, breech-loaders and QF-guns, that were altered the most. These coastal weapons were augmented by other adjuncts: searchlights, boom defences and minefields.

Graphic reconstruction of Fort St Elmo and the Carafa enceinte as it would have appeared in 1798

1. Cavalier of Fort St Elmo
2. St John Bastion
3. St Scholastica Curtain
4. Lighthouse (1633)
5. Piazza with barracks
6. Right demi-bastion (Post of Colonel Mas in 1565)
7. Porta del Soccorso
8. St Ubaldesca Curtain
9. Conception Bastion
10. St Gregory Curtain
11. Rock-hewn ditch
12. St Gregory Demi-bastion
13. Pinto Stores
14. Water cistern
15. Vendôme Bastion (1614)
16. Main landward gate (17th c.)

The Carafa Enceinte consists of elements 8, 2, 3, 9, 10 and 12.

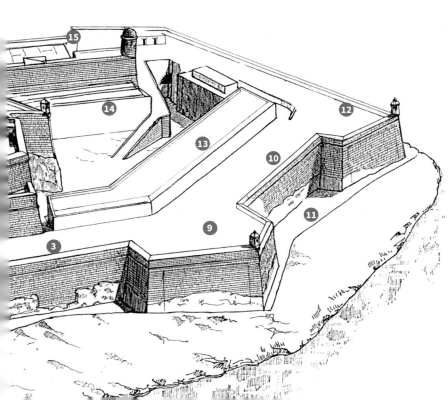

Above: The Porta del Soccorso, originally the main gate of the fort.
Right: Aerial view from the land front and ditch of Fort St Elmo facing Valletta, with its glacis formed from a series of underground granaries (*fosos*).
Below: View of the Marsamxett side of the enceinte of Fort St Elmo and its cavalier with Vendôme Bastion (lower right corner).

Above: Projected flank of right demi-bastion with 19th century British musketry parapet.
Left: low-level aerial view of land front showing the spur of the demi-bastion and paved glacis with granaries.
Below: Coffered ceiling of the chapel of Fort St Elmo.

Aerial view of Fort St Elmo, its cavalier and the enveloping apron of ramparts built by Grand Master Carafa to the design of Don Carlos de Grunenburg, showing the various structures and gun emplacements, and barracks from both the Hospitaller and later British periods.

6 | SENGLEA

SENGLEA (ISLA) – CITTÀ INVICTA

Map 1 – L10, L11
1556, 17th c.

The fortified city of Senglea developed from a small fort first erected on site in 1552. This fort was built in response to a swift Turkish raid on the island, which had caught the Knights unprepared and exposed the vulnerability of their town of Birgu to attack from the flanks. Fort St Michael, as the small stronghold was called, was eventually incorporated as the cavalier of a new bastioned enceinte designed to envelope the whole Senglea peninsula and transform it into a second fortified town during the brief reign of Grand Master Claude de la Sengle, to whom the city owes its name. Apart from its defensive value, the creation of the

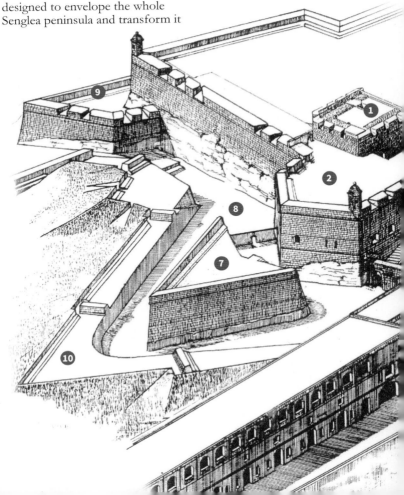

new town of Senglea was a logical and practical development that helped extend further urbanization in the harbour area and ease the congestion in Birgu. The new works progressed slowly and were still largely incomplete by 1565, the year of the Great Siege. By then, most of the works facing Corradino were very low, lacking parapets and traverses.

The flank facing Birgu was also without any fortification since the two towns were intended to provide mutual protection. So great was the destruction wrought by the Turks that after the siege Francesco Laparelli recommended that it should be razed to the ground. Although his proposal was then ignored, the defences of Senglea were only brought to a reasonable state of defence by 1581. Thereafter little was done to maintain and improve these fortifications. Various outworks were eventually added to

the land-front defences throughout the course of the seventeenth and eighteenth centuries, but the fortress had by then lost its front-line military significance as it was enclosed within two vast outer enceintes of fortification known as the Sta Margherita and Cottonera Lines.

Graphic reconstruction of Senglea's land front fortifications as these stood in 1798

1. Cavalier (Fort St Michael)
2. St Michael Bastion
3. St Anne Gate (late 17th c.)
4. Casemated rampart with flanking battery
5. Casemated rampart (Maċina)
6. Couvre Porte Battery (demolished)
7. Ravelin (17th c.) (demolished)
8. Land-front ditch
9. Counterguard (demolished)
10. Covertway with place-of-arms (18th c.) (demolished)

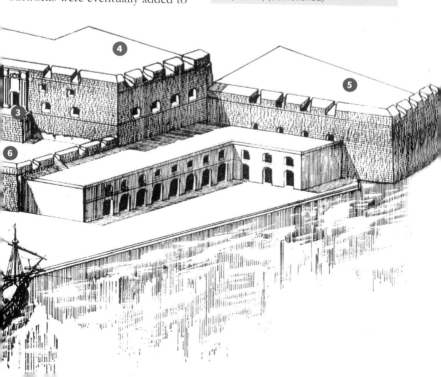

Various aerial views of Senglea's fortifications:

Top left: The spur of Senglea and its sea-level battery added by Carlos de Grunenburg in the late 1600s.

Above: View of the spur of Senglea and the Corradino-facing enceinte, with Fort St Angelo and Birgu behind it in the background.

Left: The land front of Senglea still bearing the damage suffered by aerial bombing in WWII.

Below: The casemated St Michael Bastion forming the centre of the land front with the remains of the cavalier visible beneath the clock-tower.

7 VALLETTA
VALLETTA

Map 1 – K10, L10

1566, 1640, 1680s/ 1715

Reconstructed chapel of St Roche on St Michael Counterguard.

Valletta, named after its founder, Grand Master of the Order of St John, Jean de Valette, was begun after the Great Siege in 1566 with the financial help of a Christendom grateful for the defeat of the

its strongest defences were laid out across the highest part of the promontory and comprised four strong bastions, two cavaliers and a deep rock-hewn ditch.

The new city within the fortified enclosure was built to a grid pattern with a systematic distribution and division of streets, piazzas, and pomerium. Laparelli's design also incorporated an arsenal and a *manderaggio* (galley pen) which, however, were never built. With a workforce of around 4,000 men labouring feverishly on the project, the new city of the Order was in a position to transfer its convent and seat of government there from the old town of Birgu in 1571. By the turn of the sixteenth century, Valletta had grown into the largest and most

Ottoman war machine. The new fortress was designed by the papal engineer Francesco Laparelli and incorporated most of the ingredients of the Italian bastioned system of fortification. Stretched out over the Sciberras peninsula,

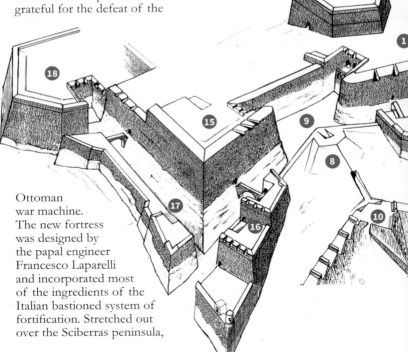

populated city on the island, with a cosmopolitan population.

The design of the fortress of Valletta remained practically unchanged from the way it was designed by Laparelli. The only alterations which were undertaken in the course of the seventeenth and eighteenth centuries were mainly designed to supply it with sorely lacking outworks in the form of four large counterguards built along the land front and the enclosure of the northern tip of the peninsula, including Fort St Elmo, within a vast apron of bastions designed to prevent a landing from the sea.

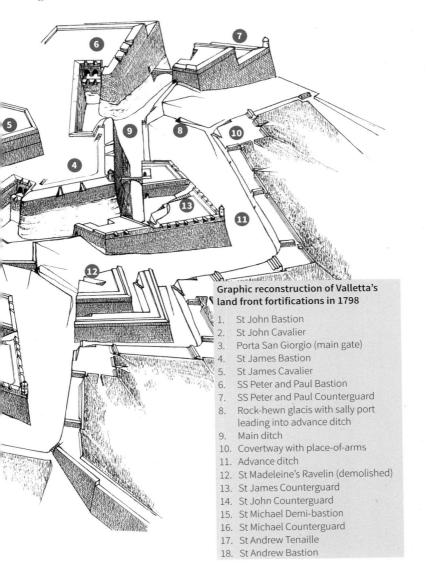

Graphic reconstruction of Valletta's land front fortifications in 1798

1. St John Bastion
2. St John Cavalier
3. Porta San Giorgio (main gate)
4. St James Bastion
5. St James Cavalier
6. SS Peter and Paul Bastion
7. SS Peter and Paul Counterguard
8. Rock-hewn glacis with sally port leading into advance ditch
9. Main ditch
10. Covertway with place-of-arms
11. Advance ditch
12. St Madeleine's Ravelin (demolished)
13. St James Counterguard
14. St John Counterguard
15. St Michael Demi-bastion
16. St Michael Counterguard
17. St Andrew Tenaille
18. St Andrew Bastion

Above: Aerial view of the Carafa enceinte with Fort St Elmo.
Right: The bastioned land front of Valletta with its counterguards and what survives of its outworks and glacis.
Below: Orillion of St James Bastion.
Below right: Aerial view of the Upper Barrakka and Lascaris Battery (19th c.).

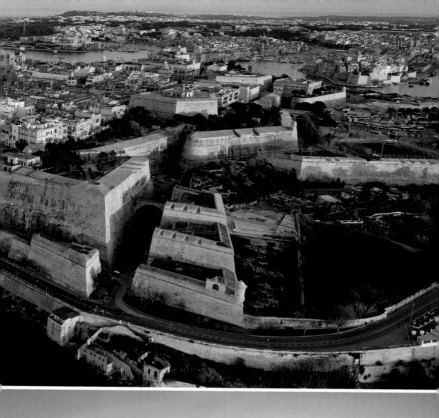

Above: Aerial view of the Marsamxett end of the land front.
Bottom: The Grand Harbour enceinte with Lascaris Battery in the foreground.

8 FLORIANA LINES

FLORIANA

Map 1 – K10

1635, 1670, 1715

The Floriana Lines were conceived in order to provide further protection to the Valletta land front. They were designed by the Italian engineer Pietro Paolo Floriani during the reign of Grand Master de Paule (1622–1636) following growing rumours of a Turkish attack.

Floriani believed that Valletta, at the time lacking any outworks whatsoever, was not adapted for modern warfare with its high bastions and narrow ditch, and therefore proposed a new front of bastioned fortifications projected further south at the neck of the peninsula, some 1600 metres from Fort St Elmo.

Porte des Bombes as remodelled by the British in the mid-1800s. This gate originally had one entrance (see overleaf) and was known as Porta dei Cannoni, although it was also commonly referred to as Porte des Bombes.

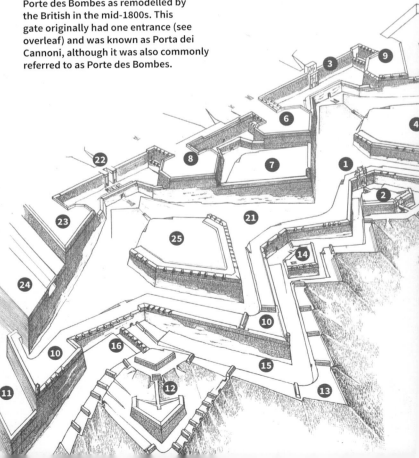

Work on the fortifications commenced in 1635 and despite the doubts expressed in Floriani's project after he departed from Malta, work on the Floriana Lines progressed quite faithfully to the original plans. A second important stage began with the arrival in 1670 of Count Antonio Maurizio Valperga, chief military architect to the house of Savoy, who proposed the construction of a braye and a crowned hornwork. By 1700 the Floriana fortifications were still unfinished, and it was only with the arrival of a French military mission that work received a fresh impetus and was brought to completion.

Graphic reconstruction of the Floriana land-front enceinte in 1798

1. Porta dei Cannoni (18th c.)
2. Ferretti Lunette with Porte des Bombes (18th c.) (demolished)
3. St Anne Gate (demolished) and Curtain
4. St Francis Ravelin
5. St Francis Bastion
6. St Luke Bastion
7. St Philip Bastion
8. St James Bastion
9. St Mark Bastion
10. Faussebraye (1670)
11. Basso Forte della Conception (1670)
12. Pietà Lunette (18th c.)
13. Covertway with place-of-arms and traverses (18th c.)
14. Lunettes (18th c.)
15. Advance Ditch
16. Battery in Advance Ditch (18th c.)
17. Hornwork (1670)
18. Crownwork (1670)
19. Ravelin
20. Spur musketry gallery (18th c.)
21. Main ditch
22. Notre Dame Gate and Curtain
23. San Salvatore Bastion
24. San Salvatore Counterguard
25. Notre Dame Ravelin

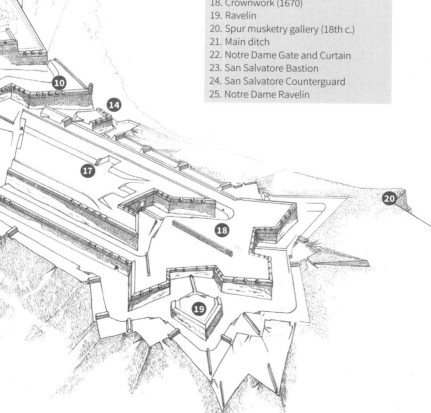

Above: The Bassoforte della Conception and the Floriana faussebraye.
Top left: Aerial view of the Floriana land front fortifications showing the glacis, lunette, and faussebraye as well as Notre Dame Ravelin.
Centre left: Nineteenth century photograph of St Anne Gate (Porta dei Cani) with its rock-hewn tenaille – both the gate and its protective outwork were demolished.
Bottom left: Nineteenth century photograph of the original Porta dei Cannoni, with its single entrance, and arched bridge leading to it.
Below: Aerial view of the crowned hornworks, known as *La Galdiana*.

9 STA MARGHERITA LINES
BORMLA (COSPICUA)

Map 1 – L11
1638, 18th c.

The Sta Margherita and Cottonera
Lines represent the two most
ambitious works of fortification
undertaken by the Knights of St
John in Malta. Begun in 1638 by
the Italian military engineer, the
Dominican Vincenzo Maculano
da Firenzuola, the Sta Margherita
Lines were designed to seal off
the high ground overlooking the
fortresses of Birgu and Senglea,
thereby denying an invading army
the ability to lay siege to the main
positions in the Grand Harbour.

**Above: St Helen Gate, the main entrance
into Bormla (Cospicua).
Below: Verdala Gate with trophy-of-arms.**

Firenzuola's enceinte, however,
was soon abandoned and remained
unfinished until well into the
eighteenth century, when the works
were taken up again, this time under
the direction of French military
engineers and brought to their
present plan. By then, however, the
Sta Margherita (Firenzuola) Lines
had lost their front-line importance
as the position had been enclosed
within a larger outer enceinte,
known as the Cottonera Lines,
begun by Grand Master Nicholas
Cotoner in 1670.

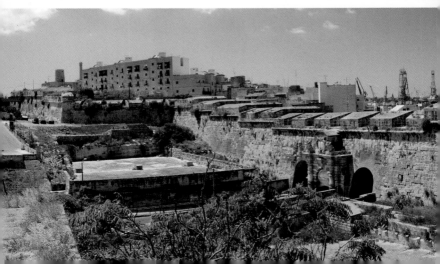

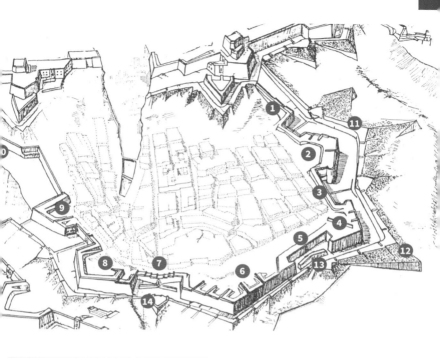

Graphic reconstruction of the Sta Margherita (Firenzuola) Lines as these stood in 1798

1. Wing with Kalkara Gate
2. Firenzuola Bastion
3. Curtain with gateway
4. Sta Margherita Bastion
5. Verdala Curtain with gateway
6. St Helen Bastion
7. St Helen Curtain and Gate
8. St John Almoner Bastion
9. St Francis Bastion (demolished)
10. St Raphael Demi-bastion (demolished)
11. Covertway with place-of-arms and traverses
12. Spur of the glacis
13. Tenaille
14. Lunette and tenaille (demolished)

Front view of the stepped curtain known as St Helen Curtain, with its main gate.

Left: Aerial view of St Helen's Curtain and its flanking bastions.
Below: A panoramic aerial view of the Sta Margherita (Firenzuola) enceinte as it stands today, missing a number of bastions and curtains which were swept away to make room for industrial development. The central element in the enceinte was converted into British fortified barracks, called Fort Verdala, in the mid-nineteenth century.

10 COTTONERA LINES

BORMLA, FGURA, PAOLA, BIRGU, KALKARA

Map 1 – L11

1670

Notre Dame (Ħaż-Żabbar) Gate.

The Cottonera Lines represent the most ambitious work of fortification undertaken by the Knights of St John in Malta. Begun in 1670, they were designed to seal off the high ground overlooking the fortresses of Birgu and Senglea, thereby denying an invading army the ability to lay siege to the main positions in the Grand Harbour.

The Cottonera Lines were begun as a direct result of the fall of Venetian Candia to the Turks in 1669 and the alarm that this event caused in Hospitaller Malta. Consisting of a massive trace of eight large bastions, encircling the earlier yet still unfinished Sta Margherita enceinte, these works were so named after Grand Master Nicholas Cotoner, who commissioned the project. The Cottonera enceinte was designed by the Italian engineer Antonio Maurizio Valperga as part of his

overall scheme for the defence of the harbours around Valletta.

Work on these fortifications began in August 1670 and continued incessantly for a decade until the death of the grand master in 1680, by which time the main body of the enceinte had already been laid down under the supervision of Mederico Blondel, the Order's resident engineer.

The funds allocated for the Cottonera fortifications had by then run out and the new grand master ordered the cessation of the project. As a result, the ravelins and cavaliers, together with the ditch and the covertway that were originally proposed by Valperga, were never constructed. The project

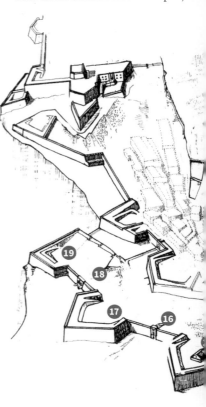

remained virtually abandoned until well into the eighteenth century, when some effort was made to bring the works to some degree of completion as an unbroken trace of ramparts and bastions.

Graphic reconstruction of the Cottonera enceinte in 1798

1. St Laurence Demi-bastion
2. Salvatore Gate
3. Fort Salvatore
4. St Louis Curtain and Gate
5. St Louis Bastion
6. St James Curtain and Gate
7. St James Bastion
8. Notre Dame Curtain and Gate
9. Partially hewn ditch
10. Notre Dame Bastion
11. St Clement Bastion
12. St Clement Curtain and Gate
13. St Nicholas Bastion
14. *Polverista* (Roccatagliata) Curtain and sally port
15. St John Bastion
16. St John Curtain and Gate
17. St Paul Bastion
18. St Paul Curtain and Gate (demolished)
19. Valperga Bastion (demolished)

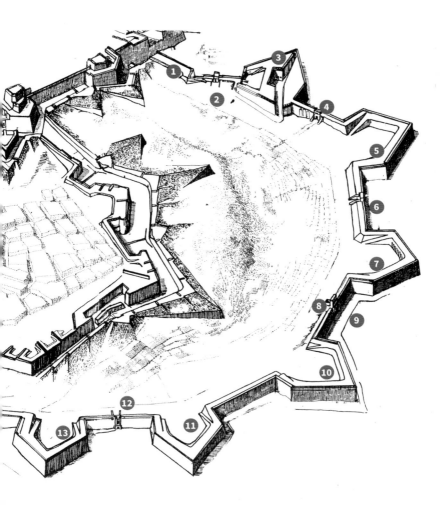

Above from left: St Paul Gate (demolished) ①, St John Gate ②, St Clement Gate ③.

Above from left: St James Gate ④ , St Louis Gate ⑤ , Salvatore Gate ⑥ .

Panoramic aerial view of the Cottonera enceinte with St Clement Retrenchment (centre).
⑦ Notre Dame Gate

Above: View of a section of the Cottonera enceinte showing St Nicholas Bastion and its adjoining ramparts. To the right is St Clement Gate.
Right: Aerial view of Notre Dame Gate with its large *corpo di guardia*. Originally the gate was served by a drawbridge and protected by a ditch and a small tenaille.
Below: Aerial view from the south east.

FORT SALVATORE
KALKARA

Map 1 – L11
1724

By the early decades of the eighteenth century, the incomplete state of the Cottonera enceinte and the open nature of its large bastions came to be considered as the main weaknesses in the defence of this massive lines of fortifications.

One of the solutions put forward to help reinforce the Cottonera fortifications was to seal off the gorges of some of the bastions with retrenchments. At Salvatore Bastion, the military engineers chose not only to retrench the bastion but to convert it into veritable fort.

Work on Fort Salvatore was begun in 1724 under the supervision of Mondion. The main casemated front, consisting of a short curtain flanked by two demi-bastions, was cut into the body of the bastion in the form of a retrenchment that practically divided the bastion into two parts. The fort itself was designed as an 'open work' to enable the defenders in Birgu to fire directly into its interior. In 1761 French engineers even recommended that this fort be

Above: Aerial view of Fort Salvatore (1724).
Below: Main gate into Fort Salvatore.

mined to prevent it from falling to the enemy and being turned against Birgu. By 1788 Fort Salvatore was armed with four 4-pdr iron guns. During World War One it was used as a prisoner-of-war camp.

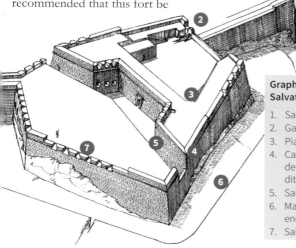

Graphic reconstruction of Fort Salvatore in 1798

1. Salvatore Gate and sally port
2. Gate into Fort Salvatore
3. Piazza (parade ground) of fort
4. Casemated front with two demi-bastions fronted by ditch cut into the bastion
5. Sally port opening into ditch
6. Main ditch of the Cottonera enceinte
7. Salvatore Bastion

12 FORT RICASOLI
KALKARA

Map 1 – L10

1670, 1715, 1780s, 19th c., 20th c.

Fort Ricasoli, begun in 1670, was the last fort built by the Knights for the protection of the Grand Harbour. It was erected to secure the promontory known as Gallows Point, a strategic site that commanded the entrance into the anchorage. Fort Ricasoli was designed by the military engineer Antonio Maurizio Valperga and named after the knight Fra Giovanni Francesco Ricasoli, who financed a large part of the project.

During the eighteenth century the Knights and their engineers invested considerable efforts in upgrading the outworks of the fort, fitting it with a covertway and a countermined glacis. The arrival of Napoleon in 1798 found the fort in a sufficiently good state of repair to have enabled its garrison to repel a number of assaults by the French troops in the short period of time before the Order was forced to capitulate.

The British immediately appreciated the importance of the fort and armed it strongly. Early during the first decade of British presence in Malta, Fort Ricasoli was the scene of a ferocious mutiny by a regiment of foreign troops, the Froberg Regiment, as a result of which a considerable section of the fort's land front was demolished when the mutineers blew up the main powder magazine. Throughout the nineteenth and twentieth centuries, the seaward bastions of the fort underwent considerable modifications to accommodate a succession of coastal guns.

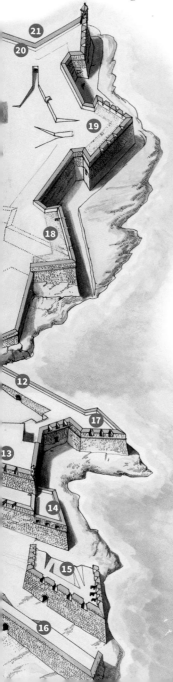

The main gate of Fort Ricasoli with its Solomonic columns was partly rebuilt after WWII. The accompanying Governor's House was also demolished but was not reconstructed.

Graphic reconstruction of Fort Ricasoli as it would have stood in 1798

1. Main gate with Governor's House
2. St John Demi-bastion
3. St Francis Bastion
4. Curtain with sally port
5. Faussebraye
6. Caponier of communication
7. Right Ravelin
8. Covertway with place-of-arms and traverses
9. Countermined glacis
10. Main ditch
11. Left Ravelin
12. Sally port
13. St Dominic Demi-bastion
14. Battery
15. Counterguard
16. Extension of covertway
17. Small bastion (No. 4 Bast. British period)
18. Battery (No. 3 Bast. British period)
19. Bastion (No. 2 Bast. British period)
20. Tenaille trace
21. Orsi Tower and battery (hidden from view)
22. St Nicholas Church
23. Brig. de Tigné's proposed retrenchment

Above: Aerial view of the seaward extremity of the land front of Fort Ricasoli showing the ruined counterguard and remains of outworks.
Left: Church of St Nicholas.
Below: Aerial view of the land front's bastioned trace.

Right: Detail of the land front of Fort Ricasoli showing three vaulted embrasures of a battery extension.

Left: View from the rear of the ruins of St Dominic Counterguard showing the sally port leading to its interior and the counterscarp in the background. This outwork has been largely eaten away by the sea.
Below: Aerial view of the salient ramparts at the tip of Fort Ricasoli, commanding the entrance to the Harbour.

13 FORT MANOEL
MANOEL ISLAND

Map 1 – K9
1723, 19th c.

Financed by the then grand master, Antonio Manoel de Vilhena, in whose honour it was named, Fort Manoel was designed as a classic square fort with four corner bastions, a ravelin, a tenaille, a covertway, and a glacis. Its low silhouette system of bastioned trace, making the widest use of crossfire to sweep the approaches, together with its aggressive outworks and countermines, was then in line with the established theories in the science of fortification. So impressive was the fort that in 1761, a delegation of visiting French military engineers, called

At the end of the seventeenth century, the Grand Harbour was more or less well protected, but the western side of Valletta was still susceptible to bombardment and attack, for the harbour of Marsamxett was devoid of any form of fortification. The greatest threat posed to Valletta was seen to come from the Isolotto, a small leaf-shaped island on which was located the quarantine hospital.

Many military engineers had pointed out this threat once the strategic value of this little island had begun to emerge with the construction of Valletta. The earliest scheme to fortify the Isolotto appears to have been first proposed in 1569, and repeated frequently throughout the course of the seventeenth century, but it was not before 1723 that work was actually commenced on a fort. Originally designed by the French engineer René Jacob de Tigné in 1715, the final design of Fort Manoel, as it was named, was produced by Charles François de Mondion, during his term as the Order's resident military engineer in charge of works of fortification and defence.

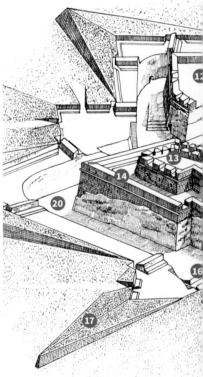

to review the island's fortifications in preparation for an impending attack, described it as a 'model du fortification fait avec soin'.

Graphic reconstruction of Fort Manoel in 1798

1. Main gate with gatecourt
2. Couvre Porte
3. St Anthony Bastion
4. Gunpowder magazine on St Helen Bastion
5. St Helen Bastion
6. Bronze statue of Grand Master de Vilhena (removed – now in Floriana)
7. Barrack block
8. Chapel of St Anthony of Padua
9. Casemated cavalier curtain with bombproof accommodation
10. St John Cavalier
11. St John Bastion
12. Ravelin
13. Notre Dame Cavalier
14. Notre Dame Bastion
15. Covertway with place-of-arms and traverses
16. Caponier of communication
17. Spur of glacis
18. Countermined glacis
19. *Polverista* on St Anthony Bastion (demolished)
20. Rock-hewn ditch

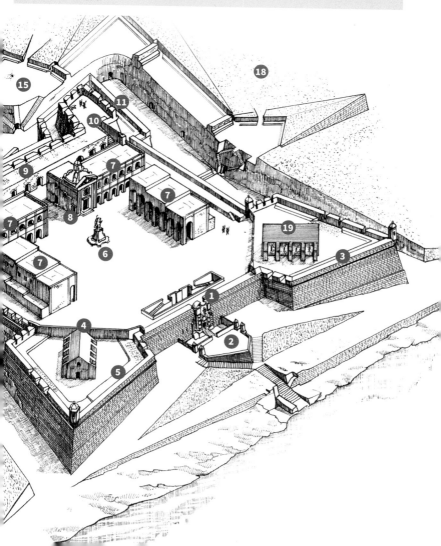

Above: The bastioned land front of Fort Manoel showing the low cavaliers joined by a curtain as well as the rock-hewn tenaille in the ditch.

Above: The bastioned seafront of Fort Manoel with its open piazza and barrack complex
Below left: The baroque main gate of Fort Manoel with its drop-ditch and sally port.
Below right: The *cantina* (pit) of the drawbridge with a working reconstruction of the wooden *tavolatura* (platform).

Above: A Vauban-style gunpowder magazine (*polverista*) with its distinctive lateral counterforts on St Helen Bastion.

Above left: The gatecourt and the lunette (couvre porte) defending the main gate into the fort.
Above right: The restored church of St Anthony of Padua.
Below: Detail of one of the bombproof masonry casemates inside the cavalier.

Aerial view of Fort Manoel and its outworks. The glacis was planted over with shrubs and trees in the 1970s. An anti-aircraft battery was built on the covertway and glacis in WWII. Other British-period alterations and additions to the fort are the metal bridge spanning the ditch near the salient of St John Bastion and the 12-pdr QF Battery on St Anthony Bastion.

14 FORT CHAMBRAI

GĦAJNSIELEM, GOZO

Map 1 – N5

1749

The proposal for the building of a new fortified city in Gozo, to replace the old and landlocked castle, was put forward many times during the 17th century.

It was revived during the reign of Grand Master Perellos in 1715, when the French military mission headed by Brig. René Jacob de Tigné suggested that a stronghold be erected at Ras it-Tafal (Rasetafal) overlooking Mġarr Harbour. The first project was approved in 1722, designed by Charles François de

Mondion, but it was only begun many years later when Balì Jacques François de Chambrai offered to finance the project himself in 1749, during the reign of Grand Master Pinto de Fonseca.

Francesco Marandon, the Order's resident engineer, was dispatched to Gozo and tasked with the building and supervision of the work. Fort Chambrai was originally designed as a fortified city for the protection of the Gozitan inhabitants. The town planned to be established within its walls was to be laid out on a grid

General layout of Fort Chambrai's fortifications as these would have stood around 1798

1. St Anthony Bastion
2. Land-front ditch
3. Main gate
4. Advance gate
5. Right ravelin
6. St Paul Bastion
7. Counterguard
8. Curtain
9. Notre Dame Bastion
10. Left ravelin
11. Covertway with place-of-arms
12. Guardian Angel Bastion (two-tiered)
13. *Polverista* (gunpowder magazine)
14. Echaugette

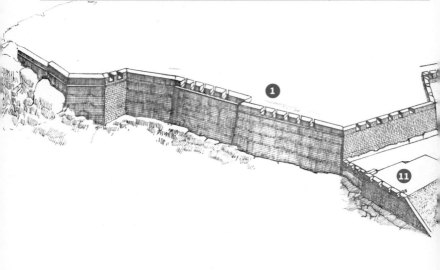

pattern of square blocks, avenues, and streets but the settlement was never established and the fort remained a purely military establishment.

Its main defences consist of a bastioned land front enveloped by a ditch, covertway and glacis, two long flanks, and an unfortified cliff face along the southern part of the plateau.

Echaugette or *gardjola* (sentry box) with its bellcot overlooking the cove at ix-Xatt l-Aħmar, Gozo.

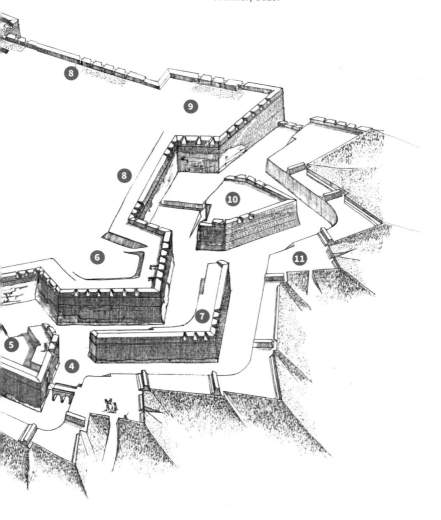

Above: Cliff face along the southern part of the enceinte of the plateau originally known as Ras it-Tafal.
Left: Aerial view of Guardian Angel Bastion with its conical gunpowder magazine.
Below: Aerial view of the land front of Fort Chambrai showing the remains of the covertway and glacis.

Above: The conical gunpowder magazine on Guardian Angel Bastion.
Below right: View of the Advance Gate and bridge in the left face of the right ravelin.
Bottom right: The main Baroque gate, crowned with the coat of arms of Grand Master Pinto, and its original arched bridge spanning the ditch.

15 FORT TIGNÉ
TAS-SLIEMA

Map 1 – L9
1792–1793, 19th c., 1937

major work of fortification built by the Order in Malta. In plan it consisted of a central, diamond-shaped casemated body with detached tower-keep to the rear, pierced with two rows of musketry loopholes, all enclosed within a wide ditch flanked by three counterscarp musketry galleries and a countermined glacis.

Considerable alterations to the original design were made during the nineteenth and early twentieth centuries, when the British military

Fort Tigné was begun in 1793 and was a very small work by eighteenth-century standards, actually more of a large redoubt. However, its design was probably the most revolutionary and influential of all the fortifications built by the Knights in Malta. Designed by the Order's then chief engineer, Antoine-Etienne de Tousard, its most important features were the lack of bastions and the counterscarp musketry galleries.

The design was heavily influenced by the writings of Montalembert and more particularly by the lunettes built by the French general, Jean-Claude Lemichaud d'Arçon in places such as Mont Dauphin. By the end of the eighteenth century, the supremacy of the bastioned system was being challenged by the growing popularity of the tenaille trace. The new style of fortification known as the polygonal system, of which Fort Tigné is one of the earliest examples, was to dominate the art of military architecture through most of the following century. Fort Tigné was the last

strove to adapt the work to a succession of increasingly larger and more modern heavy armament, beginning with the heavy RML guns, Brennen torpedoes, QF and BL guns, most of which had to be fitted outside the fort on the glacis, due to the small size of the fort.

The beginning of the twentieth century saw Fort Tigné armed with two 9.2-inch BL coastal defence guns, which were then replaced in the late 1930s with a battery of three 6-inch BL guns.

Graphic reconstruction of Fort Tigné in 1798

1. Circular tower-keep (*tour-reduit*)
2. Main gate
3. Caponier
4. Masonry flight of steps
5. Ditch
6. Counterscarp musketry gallery
7. Courtyard
8. Defensible barrack block
9. Casemated flank with parapet and embrasures
10. Musketry scarp gallery
11. Countermined glacis

Above: Aerial view of Fort Tigné, with its British battery (Tigné Battery – 1937) and other additions, including the masonry escarpment.
Below left: The circular tower-keep (*tour-reduit*) of Fort Tigné with its two tiers of musketry loopholes.
Below right: Reconstructed flight of steps linking the fort to the foreshore.

Above: The main entrance into the tower-keep.
Below: Defensible barrack block (*abris*) inside the fort with its reconstructed wooden bridge linking it to the tower keep.
Bottom: Aerial view of Fort Tigné with the coastal battery added in 1937.

THE BASTIONED TOWERS (*FORTINI*)

The first coastal defences built by the Knights were large squarish towers sometimes referred to as *fortini* (small forts). The first to materialize was Garzes Tower, built in 1605 at Mġarr, Gozo. This was followed by six towers built by Grand Master Alof de Wignacourt.

These were erected at St Paul's Bay (1609/1610); Marsaxlokk (St Lucian Tower – 1610); St Thomas Bay, Marsaskala (1614); Marsalforn, Gozo (1616); Comino (St Mary Tower – 1618); and Sta Maria delle Grazie (1620). These towers were large squarish structures that were fitted (with one exception – Gozo) with bastioned corner turrets. These massive structures were built to dominate the coastline, with their batteries of heavy artillery mounted on their roofs. They were also garrisoned by sizeable detachments of troops in times of emergency.

Internally, all the towers contained large barrel-vaulted rooms, built a *prova di bomba*. Such towers proved very expensive to build and none were erected after the mid-1600s, when the Knights opted for smaller and cheaper lookout posts instead.

Example of a bastioned tower – St Thomas Bay Tower, Marsaskala. In 1715, most of these towers were fitted with external semicircular gun batteries to increase their fire power.

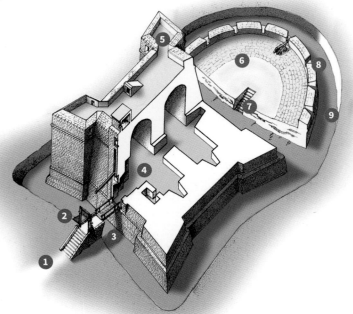

1. Flight of steps leading up to entrance, connected by a drawbridge
2. Wooden palisade (*rastello*)
3. Rock-hewn ditch
4. Vaulted interior rooms
5. Corner turret/bastion
6. External semicircular battery (1715)
7. Steps
8. Parapet
9. Rock-hewn ditch of battery

ST PAUL'S BAY TOWER
ST PAUL'S BAY

Map 1 – F6

1609–1610

Wignacourt Tower is the first of the coastal towers built in Malta by Grand Master Alof de Wignacourt. The first stone was laid with due ceremony on 10 February 1610. Its design has often been attributed to the Maltese architect Vittorio Cassar, but this claim is nowadays discredited owing to the fact that Cassar is now known to have died before the tower was even proposed.

The stout and strongly built structure is defined by its four corner turrets, two of which, facing inland, were fitted with guardrooms. Internally the tower consisted of two vaulted rooms and its main entrance was set on the first floor, originally reached via an external flight of steps and across a wooden drawbridge (both of which are now missing). A small seaward-facing battery was added in 1715. In 1761 it was found necessary to reinforce two of its walls with a buttressing revetment. Among the original fixtures of the tower still to be seen *in situ* are its heavy wooden door and the remains of its drawbridge – lifting mechanism.

Above: Wignacourt Tower at St Paul's Bay with its original external masonry flight of steps before this was removed. A small gun platform was added to the seaward side of the tower in 1715 (top image).

2 ST LUCIAN TOWER
MARSAXLOKK

Map 1 – M14

1610, 1872

St Lucian Tower enclosed by the British-built coastal fort in 1872.

St Lucian Tower was begun in 1610 and was paid for by Grand Master Alof de Wignacourt. It was a powerful, solidly built structure fitted with corner turrets and capable of mounting heavy guns on its roof. Originally its main entrance was served by an external masonry flight of steps and a wooden drawbridge (now both missing).

This tower was the main defensive element in Marsaxlokk harbour until 1715, when the anchorage was fitted with a system of batteries, redoubts and entrenchments. The tower, too, in fact, underwent its first of a series of alterations when it was fitted out with a strong, seaward facing, semicircular gun platform. Later, in 1795, both the tower and this battery were enclosed by a ditch and the whole complex rechristened Fort Rohan in honour of the then Grand Master Emmanuel De Rohan-Polduc.

This fortified complex was actually one of the few Hospitaller defensive works to put up a spirited resistance against Napoleon's army when the French invaded Malta in 1798. Later, during the Anglo-Maltese blockade of the French garrison, the British military adopted St Lucian Tower as their main supply base and fallback position. In 1874 the British military enclosed the tower within the perimeter of a coastal fort designed to house three 10-inch of 18-ton RML guns and their magazines, giving the structure the appearance it has today.

ST THOMAS BAY TOWER
MARSASKALA

Map 1 – O12

1614, 1715

St Thomas Tower differed significantly from its two predecessors in the treatment of its corner turrets, which were now more pronounced and projected outwards from the faces of the tower to form veritable pentagonal bastions, giving the whole structure a distinctive four-bastioned, star-shaped plan.

Structurally, St Thomas Tower was built around two adjoining and interlinked barrel vaults, which, in the parlance of the period, rendered the tower *a prova di bomba* or bombproof. This also allowed it to mount heavy pieces of artillery on its roof, thus enabling it to serve as a coastal artillery platform. The entrance to the tower was through a vaulted doorway set within a turret located centrally in the landward face of the structure. This turret was surmounted by a guardroom which was added at a later stage, itself fitted with an external

Above: St Thomas Tower and its partly reconstructed coastal battery (added in 1715).
Bottom: The landward side of the tower with its enveloping ditch.

flagpole holder and decorated with a small marble escutcheon bearing Wignacourt's family coat of arms mounted in a boxed frame recess above the doorway.

The entrance was served by a wooden drawbridge while a shallow rock-hewn fosso, or ditch, about 10 m wide in front of the faces and 17 m wide in front of the bastion salients, enveloped the tower. In 1715 a semicircular battery was added to the seaward side of the tower.

4

ST MARY TOWER
COMINO

Map 1 – B2

1618

St Mary Tower (or Comino Tower) was the sixth of seven coastal towers built during the reign of Grand Master Wignacourt. It was begun in 1618 and cost the sum of 17,628 scudi, making it the most expensive of the coastal towers built by the Knights. For some reason Ġan Franġisk Abela, writing in 1647, misattributes its design to Vittorio Cassar. This architect is now known to have died in 1609.

St Mary Tower had many interesting features that set it distinctly apart from its sister structures. It stands 19.6 m high, some 8 m higher than the other towers. A masonry plinth, designed to reinforce the vaulted structure, projected from the base of the tower and was topped by an all-round, roofed musketry gallery. This feature, now missing, also contained the outer gate and drawbridge mechanism, which was approached by a detached flight of steps.

The tower was enveloped by a countermined glacis and a ditch.

A small sally port provided access from within the tower into the ditch. From Fra Renato de Gras' inspection of the tower in 1722 we know that the tower was armed with five guns, but it played no part in the defence of the Maltese islands during the French invasion of 1798. The structure, however, was to see service as a prison for French sympathizers during the Maltese insurrection and blockade in 1798–1800.

ST AGATHA TOWER
MELLIEHA

Map 1 – B4
1647–1649

Fort St Agatha (also known as Torre Rossa, Red Tower or Mellieha Tower) was the last of the coastal strongholds built by Grand Master Lascaris. Begun in 1647 and finished two years later, it was designed to defend Mellieha Bay and communicate with the defensive structures on the nearby islands of Gozo and Comino. This tower was designed by the French military architect Antonio Garsin, who based his plans on the earlier design of Wignacourt's bastioned towers. Its characteristic features are its four corner turrets.

The structure was solidly built with thick walls and barrel-vaulted ceilings, designed to allow it to mount heavy cannon on its roof with which to fire at enemy vessels approaching too close to the shore.

In the course of the eighteenth century, the tower was enclosed

within a redan-trace entrenchment built in the *pietra a secco* manner (dry stone walling) and used as a redoubt and rallying point for the militia troops detailed to defend Mellieha Bay.

THE LASCARIS TOWERS

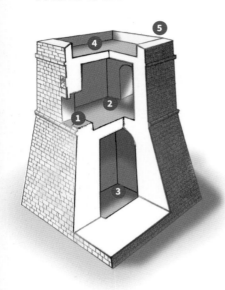

1. Entrance to tower placed on first floor and reached by rope or wooden ladder
2. Living quarters – floor resting on rib arches
3. Ground floor room used for storage and accessed internally through a trap door
4. Terrace of tower resting on wooden beams – tower was too weak to mount cannon
5. Low parapet

By the mid-seventeenth century, the Knights' preference for large garrisoned outposts was discarded in favour of small structures which were designed to serve solely as watch-posts. Six such towers were built by Grand Master Lascaris in the years between 1636 and 1657 at Għajn Tuffieħa, Lippija, St George's Bay, Nadur, and Wied iż-Żurrieq.

The design of these watchtowers reflected a marked departure from the expensive massive fortlets which had been built during Wignacourt's reign. These were specifically designed as low-cost lookout posts intended solely for the purpose of keeping a watch over the coastline, in order to warn of any approaching enemy vessels.

The Lascaris towers came in two varieties. The earliest batch were relatively tall and slender, about 11 m high and about 6 m² in plan. Internally, each consisted of two single-roomed floors with external access provided solely to the upper floor, generally reached either by a wooden ladder or rope ladder. The towers were very lightly built, however, lacking the solidity that would have been provided by a barrel-vaulted form of construction. Indeed, their terrace platform, which rested on wooden beams, could not even take the weight of a light signalling cannon.

A later and more solid version, of which two examples were erected at Wied iż-Żurrieq and St George's Bay, were built more solidly with a casemated vault to allow them to mount cannon. These were actually to serve as the blueprint for the thirteen coastal towers built later by Grand Master de Redin in 1658–1659.

The Lascaris Towers at Għajn Tuffieħa, Lippija, and Qawra Point were decorated with an escutcheon bearing the coat of arms of Grand Master Lascaris carved in low relief.

The Lascaris towers had no heavy artillery. A few of the towers, however, were armed with small calibre breech-loading guns mounted on tripods (*cavalletti*) which fired through the sea-facing windows on the first floor of the structure.

A GĦAJN TUFFIEĦA TOWER, MĠARR

Map 1 – B8

1637

E LIPPIJA TOWER, MĠARR

Map 1 – B8

B QAWRA POINT, QAWRA

Map 1 – G6

1637

F ST GEORGE'S BAY TOWER, ST JULIAN'S

Map 1 – J8

1637

C NADUR TOWER, L/O RABAT

Map 1 – D10

1637

G SCIUTA TOWER, WIED IŻ-ŻURRIEQ

Map 1 – H15

1637

D XLENDI TOWER, MUNXAR, GOZO

Map 1 – J5

1650

H DWEJRA TOWER, SAN LAWRENZ, GOZO

Map 1 – H3

1652

THE DE REDIN TOWERS

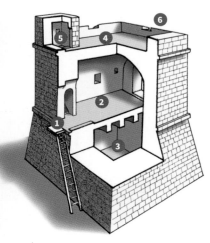

1. Entrance on first floor reached by rope or wooden ladder
2. Living quarters – floor resting on rib arches
3. Storage accessed via trap door
4. Terrace resting on barrel vault
5. Spiral staircase
6. Low parapet with embrasures

A spiral staircase provided access to the roof, where a small room served to provide some shelter to the sentinels on duty.

The towers were manned by the *Guardia Torre*, a kind of permanent guard that was paid by the Università and kept watch all year round. Each tower was provided with a small iron gun which was mounted on the roof and which was used largely for signalling purposes.

The Lascaris watchtowers were followed by another 13 towers erected in Malta in 1658–1659 at the expense of Grand Master de Redin. These towers were meant to form a visual chain of communication all around the island, and were thus positioned within visual distance of one another in order to enable signals to be relayed from one post to the next all the way down the coast to Valletta.

Work on the de Redin towers proceeded at a very fast pace so that the first tower to be built at Għajn Ħadid, near Mellieħa, was completed within two months. Structurally the de Redin towers were more sturdy than their flimsy Lascaris predecessors. Based on the two prototypes erected during Lascaris' reign at Wied iż-Żurrieq and St George's Bay, de Redin's towers were likewise built around a barrel vault and thus capable of mounting cannon. Internally, each tower consisted of two rooms connected by an opening on the first floor. This was accessed by means of a wooden ladder or rope.

I **GĦAJN ĦADID TOWER, SELMUN**
Map 1 – E5
1658

J **XROBB L-GĦAĠIN TOWER, MARSAXL**
Map 1 – O14
1659

K | **MADLIENA TOWER, MADLIENA**

Map 1 – I7

1658

O | **TRIQ IL-WIESGĦA TOWER, ĦAŻ-ŻABBAR**

Map 1 – N11

1659

L | **ST JULIAN'S TOWER, TAS-SLIEMA**

Map 1 – K9

1658

P | **ĦAMRIJA TOWER, QRENDI**

Map 1 – H15

1659

M | **AĦRAX TOWER, MELLIEĦA**

Map 1 – C3

1658

Q | **WARDIJA TOWER, ŻURRIEQ**

Map 1 – I15

1659

N | **GĦALLIS TOWER, NAXXAR**

Map 1 – G6

1658

R | **QALET MARKU TOWER, NAXXAR**

Map 1 – H6

1658

Above: Graphic reconstruction of Mġarr ix-Xini Tower showing it as it stood originally in 1661 with its box machicolations.
Below: Aerial view of San Blas (Ta' Sopu) Tower, Nadur (1667).
(Map 1 – O3)

Above: Aerial view of Xlendi Bay showing the coastal tower and its adjoining rocky escarpment.
Below: Mġarr ix-Xini Tower (1661). (Map 1 – M6)

OTHER TOWERS

Apart from the system of coastal military and signalling towers, the Maltese islands also had a number of domestic, privately owned structures which were used either as residences or for the protection of rural settlements.

A number of these structures even seem to have pre-dated the arrival of the Knights in Malta in 1530. By the late fifteenth century, with the growing threat of Muslim corsair raids, there developed a need for protective towers capable of providing some refuge for the rural settlements.

Matteo Perez D'Aleccio's map of Malta at the time of the Great Siege depicts various towers scattered around the island. Other structures, although built in the form of towers, did not have any military value.

VERDALA PALACE, RABAT

Map 1 – F12

1580s

Verdala Palace was actually a fortified country residence which Grand Master Hughes Loubenx de Verdalle built for himself at the Boschetto, and whose design Ġan Franġisk Abela attributes to Girolamo Cassar, the Order's resident engineer. Described as a *rocca* by Abela, this country villa was a veritable stronghold, surrounded with its own rock-hewn ditch and served with a drawbridge. Prof. Quentin Hughes believed that it was inspired by Vignola's Palazzo Farnese at Caprarola, begun in 1559, which Cassar probably came across during his architectural visit to Italy in 1566.

KAVALLIERI TOWER, QRENDI

Map 1 – I14

Medieval [?]

Kavallieri Tower in Qrendi appears to pre-date the arrival of the Knights to Malta. Its octagonal plan, pointed internal arches, heavy use of machicolation and total absence of gun loops, as well as the fact that it forms part of a medieval complex of buildings, seems to hint at a pre-1530 origin. Its most distinct defensive features are its eight *piombatoie* or box-machicolations, the drop-boxes known locally as the *galleriji tal-mishun*, balcony-like structures which were used for dropping projectiles and boiling oil on assailants.

CAPTAIN'S TOWER, NAXXAR

Map 1 – H9

1558

Captain's Tower (Torri tal-Kaptan), was erected during the magistracy of Grand Master Jean de Valette to house the captain of the Naxxar militia. The tower is square in plan and consists of three floors, with the rooms spanned by stone arches. Its primary defensive features were the *piombatoie*, or box-machicolations, used for dropping projectiles onto assailants at the foot of the tower. An interesting feature appertaining to this tower is a *columbarium* set within the four-foot high parapet on the roof and used to house carrier pigeons.

GAUCI TOWER, NAXXAR

Map 1 – H9

1548

This tower was built by Francesco Gauci at a cost of 400 scudi in order to safeguard his family and property against corsair raids – pirates had actually carried off Gauci's wife in the course of one of their *razzie*. The Knights tried to take it over in 1548, but Francesco petitioned Grand Master Juan d'Homedes and he was allowed to keep the structure. Gauci Tower is a stout defensive structure with a battered lower half and a ring of 12 box-machicoulis projecting from its parapet. Its walls also had an ample provision of musketry loopholes, cruciform crossbow slits, and vision slits, making it easy to defend against lightly armed marauding corsairs.

MAMO TOWER, MARSASKALA

Map 1 – N13

1657

Mamo Tower was designed in the shape of a St Andrew's Cross with four diagonally placed projecting towers that endowed it with sixteen sides. Its construction is credited to a certain Gregorio Mamo and his son Giorgio. The whole structure lacks an upper superstructure since it was not finished to its full height. As a result it lacks machicolation and other defensive features. It was, nevertheless, enveloped by a rock-hewn ditch. The structure was very solidly built around a central vaulted room – giving it the appearance of a fort.

BUBAQRA TOWER, ŻURRIEQ

Map 1 – J15

17th c.

Bubaqra Tower, situated in the limits of Żurrieq, is a fortified country residence dating to around the late sixteenth century. Its architect is unknown but the structure is said to have been built at the bequest of a local priest by the name of Matteolo Pisani. The tower has a very simple and austere cubic form, built to a square plan and crowned by four corner turrets each decorated with stepped crenellations terminating in spherical finials. Large run-off rainwater spouts, shaped in the form of cannon, project from its upper faces. The tower is surrounded by a large splendid garden. Quentin Hughes claimed that the tower was also employed at one stage by the Order as an inland defensive post.

VINCENTI TOWER, MQABBA

Map 1 – I13

18th c.

Vincenti Tower was a very high and slender structure, with two storeys on which stood a smaller tower. It was built in 1726 by Fra Orfeo de Vincenzo, a prior of the Order of St John. An escutcheon and an inscription, commemorating its construction, now lost, were affixed to one of its faces. In 1941 it was requisitioned by the British military and used as an observation post. Unfortunately, it was severely damaged in 1942 and had to be largely pulled down, leaving only the scarped ground floor standing.

SELMUN PALACE, SELMUN

Map 1 – D6

18th c.

Although given the shape of a square tower with four corner bastions in the shape of Wignacourt's towers, Selmun Palace is actually an eighteenth-century private country villa. Its exact date of construction is unknown, although it was already standing by 1783, when it is referred to as 'Torre Nuova'. This was not a military structure and had no active defensive role. Its silhouette, nevertheless, when seen from far out at sea, served as a visual deterrent.

STA CECILIA TOWER, GHAJNSIELEM

Map 1 – M5
17th c.

Sta Cecilia Tower was one of four towers which could be found around the village of Xewkija, in Gozo, by the early eighteenth century. This tower acquired its name from a nearby medieval chapel dedicated to the same saint. It is said to have been built by Bernardo Macedonia, who served as commander of artillery in 1613, and indeed his coat of arms can still be seen above the entrance to the tower. This structure has an austere external appearance, devoid of any defensive features such as drop-boxes and gun loops, common to most other towers. It is broken by a few decorative features in the form of string courses, a line of small projecting corbels and crenellations.

GHAR IL-ĠOBON TOWER, BIRKIRKARA

Map 1 – I10
17th c.

This small domestic tower, or torricella, also known as it-Torri ta' Birkirkara, situated nowadays in the midst of a heavy urban setting, is a well-preserved example of tal-mishun typology of domestic towers. Six piombatoie crown its parapet. The tower seems to date to the seventeenth century. According to A. Mifsud (Malta, 1920) the entrance to the first floor was reached by an external flight of steps.

TAL-BUTTAR TOWER, MARSASKALA

Map 1 – N12
17th c.

This large private tower, nowadays used as a farmhouse, was built with very pronounced military features. Amongst these was the provision for a heavy wooden drawbridge, served by an external flight of steps similar to those found in military towers erected by the Knights of St John. Nothing is as yet known about when and who designed and built it, but its features tend to date the tower to around the mid-seventeenth century. A secondary feature of the tower is its columbarium (dovecote), a structure intended to house pigeons or doves, which was built into the thickness of the parapet.

Bubaqra Tower, situated in the limits of Żurrieq, is a fortified country residence dating to around the late sixteenth century.

Above: Aerial view of Tal-Buttar Tower, Marsaskala.

Top right: Ta' Lanzun Tower, a fortified *massaria* type of enclosure dating back to around 1676.

Left: Zammitello Tower, situated on the outskirts of the village of Mġarr, is not a work of fortification. Despite its appearance and antiquated military features, it is just a nineteenth-century architectural folly, a product of the Victorian era. Its mixture of bartizans and turrets finds no echo in the military architecture of the Maltese islands.

Right: Ta' Bettina Tower at Xrobb l-Għaġin with an adjoining chapel dating to *c*.1751.

Below: Aerial view of the Captain's Tower at Naxxar.

Bottom right: Rustic tower near a quarry at ix-Xwieki, Naxxar.

Despite the introduction of the system of towers, the Knights did not do away with the network of unfortified and open-air militia watchposts, some stations of which had been in use since well before 1530.

Ever since the Middle Ages, the Maltese had made use of a system of *guardia coste*, known as the *maħras*, to keep watch over their islands' shores. This system came to include all the men of Malta between the ages of 16 and 65 (the clergy were exempted), who were obliged to keep watch one night a week according to an established roster.

The men were deployed in three-man groups at strategic points around the coastline at night and, in a few sensitive places, even by day. When Grand Masters Lascaris and Martin de Redin built their coastal towers in the middle of the seventeenth century, the Knights still had a network of *guardie*, many of which were out in the open, but others had small refuge places in the form of unfortified stone huts. Some of these sentry rooms soldiered well into the eighteenth century, while the Knights went on to add other militia stations of their own. However, only a couple of such *posti di guardia / corpi di guardia* are known to have survived, although more may be still be identified in the future. One of these is found at Għajn Ħadid, sitting just to the rear of the remains of the De Redin Tower. It is a simple rectangular block measuring roughly 8 x 5.5 x 4.6 m (h) while some distance away stood a small rectangular sentry box (demolished).

Another so-called 'Dejma post' often cited is the Ta' Tabibu farmhouse in St Paul's Bay. A *corp di guardia* building built in the form of a courtyard enclosure and fitted with a superstructure dating from the eighteenth century can be found at Wied Qirda, limits of Ħaż-Żebbuġ. Among its features is a pair of flagpole holders which were used to secure masts for signalling purposes.

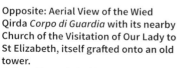

Above: Rural post at il-Bidni, l/o Ħaż-Żabbar.
Left: Sentry walk and merlon at the Wied Qirda *Corpo di Guardia*.
Below: View of the courtyard of the Wied Qirda *Corpo di Guardia*.

Opposite: Aerial View of the Wied Qirda *Corpo di Guardia* with its nearby Church of the Visitation of Our Lady to St Elizabeth, itself grafted onto an old tower.
Below: Flagpole holder and sundial on the il-Bidni post. Inscribed date near sundial reads 1743.
Bottom right: Flagpole holder and sundial on the superstructure of the Wied Qirda post.

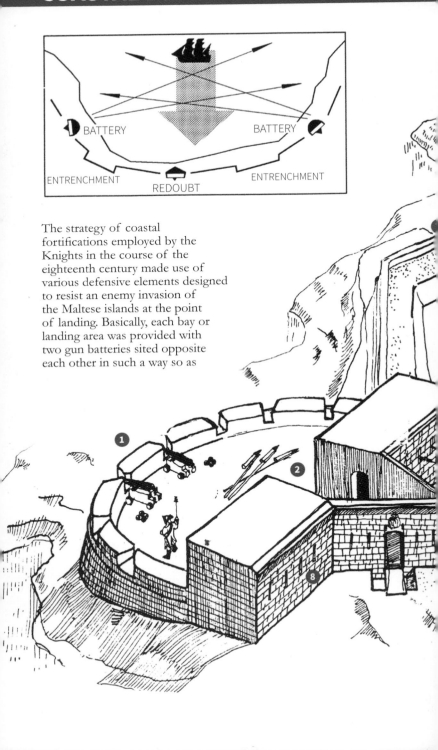

BATTERY

BATTERY

ENTRENCHMENT

ENTRENCHMENT

REDOUBT

The strategy of coastal fortifications employed by the Knights in the course of the eighteenth century made use of various defensive elements designed to resist an enemy invasion of the Maltese islands at the point of landing. Basically, each bay or landing area was provided with two gun batteries sited opposite each other in such a way so as

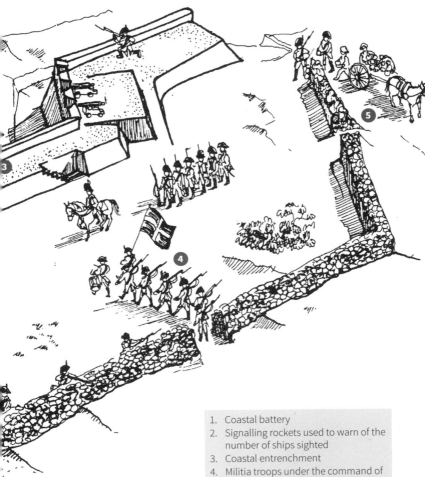

to catch enemy ships and vessels attempting to disembark their troops on shore in their crossfire (see diagram top left). Once ashore, however, the enemy soldiers would then encounter local militia troops firing their weapons from behind entrenchment walls and redoubts. After 1741 this system was augmented with the inclusion of a number of fougasses (stone-firing mortars).

1. Coastal battery
2. Signalling rockets used to warn of the number of ships sighted
3. Coastal entrenchment
4. Militia troops under the command of a knight arrive at their pre-assigned defensive positions
5. Sappers build defensive rubble walls to consolidate the rear of the defensive positions
6. Fougasses are filled with stones and fired at the approaching enemy vessels once they enter the field of fire
7. Cutting in the entrenchment wall allows for counter attacks
8. Musketry loopholes in the redan and blockhouses of the battery allow the garrison to ward off landward attacks

COASTAL BATTERIES

The brief outburst of enthusiasm shown by the Order for the fortification of the coastal areas of Malta, with the building of some 30 towers during the first half of the seventeenth century, appears to have waned considerably after 1667.

The concept of opposing the enemy on the beaches only began to find adherents again amongst the Knights around the turn of the century, particularly through the influence of the Order's French military engineers.

The first proposal for coastal batteries began to appear in 1714, and by 1715 this had quickly developed into an ambitious island-wide network of batteries. The scheme found a stout adherent in the prior of France, Philippe de Vendôme, and it was particularly because of his financial support that these defences were able to materialize. Indeed, between 1715 and 1716, work on the coastal fortifications consumed a total of 41,561 scudi.

The coastal batteries built by the Knights of St John followed a pattern evolved by the French at the end of the seventeenth century and consisted, basically, of gun-platforms ringed by embrasured parapets with one or two defensible blockhouses closing off the rear.

Various combinations of these features were employed, leading to the creation of a great variety of battery designs. Most of the structures were built in the years 1715–1716, but a few others were added in the course of the 1730s and 1750s, with the last battery being constructed in 1792 at Delimara Point (this has not survived).

1. Redan with main entrance into battery
2. Musketry loopholes in redan
3. Defensive blockhouse
4. Parapet with embrasures facing the sea
5. Shallow ditch fronting battery on seaward side
6. Low parapet en barbette with paved gun platform

QAWRA POINT BATTERY, QAWRA

Map 1 – G6
1715

Qawra Point Battery occupied a very important strategic position at the entrance to Salina Bay and the salt pans located therein. It was built around an already existing tower erected during Grand Master Lascaris' magistracy. The battery consisted of a roughly semicircular platform with elongated sides, with two blockhouses and a redan protecting the landward approaches and main entrance. The battery was also enveloped by a shallow

rock-hewn ditch. Adjoining the battery stood a short stretch of coastal entrenchment wall.

WESTREME BATTERY, MELLIEĦA

Map 1 – C5
1715, 1939

Westreme Battery, or Mellieħa Right Battery as it was also known, was an important defensive element and one of the many features defending the large anchorage at Mellieħa. This battery differs from many of its sister batteries in the fact that it had only one small blockhouse, and this was placed diagonally across the gorge of the platform, so that two of its outer faces served as a redan. A high boundary wall, fitted with a

small door, sealed off the rest of the battery. The blockhouse was adapted for coastal defence in WWII.

ST MARY BATTERY, COMINO

Map 1 – B2
1715

St Mary Battery, overlooking the Malta-Comino channel, is one of the best preserved coastal batteries in the Maltese islands. It was begun in 1714, and the considerable sum of 850 scudi had already been expended on its construction by 1715, when the Knights decided to relocate it to its present site. The battery has a semicircular gun-platform with a thick masonry parapet pierced by 8 embrasures, and a diagonally-mounted blockhouse with adjoining walls,

pierced with loopholes closing off the rear. In 1785 this work was armed with six iron cannon (two 24-pdr and four 6-pdr).

4 WIED MUSA BATTERY, MARFA

Map 1 – B4

1715

Also known as Swatar Battery, Wied Musa Battery was begun in 1714 and cost a total of 938 scudi when completed in 1716. Commander Mongontier had donated 250 scudi towards its construction in 1714. In plan, the battery consisted of a roughly semicircular platform fitted with a parapet pierced by four embrasures. A large blockhouse, fitted with musketry loopholes and originally protected by a redan (now missing), defended the landward approaches. Wied Musa Battery had no ditch. By 1785 it was armed with four 8-pdr iron guns. Its complement of gunpowder was kept at Mellieha Tower.

5 ARRIAS BATTERY, XEMXIJA

Map 1 – E6

1715

Also known as St Paul's Bay Left Battery, this battery was named in honour of Bailiff Emanuel Arrias, who contributed financially towards its construction. An inscription gives the date of its completion as 1716, by which time it had consumed the sum of 737 scudi. The battery had an elongated plan, with a rectangular blockhouse to the rear, its parapet pierced by only one embrasure, since most of its six 6-pdr guns were mounted en barbette. By 1785 three of its guns had been removed and its stock of gunpowder was kept at Mellieha Tower.

6 QOLLA L-BAJDA BATTERY, GOZO

Map 1 – K1

1715

Qolla l-Bajda Battery has a semicircular platform with two blockhouses enclosing the rear. The work lacked a redan, but musketry loopholes in the flanks of the blockhouses allowed the defenders to protect the approaches to the main entrance on the landward side of the work. The battery had six embrasures opening in its parapet and was armed, in 1770, with four 6-pdr iron guns. This battery, given its distant and isolated location, kept its own store of gunpowder.

MISTRA BATTERY, MISTRA

Map 1 – E6
1714, 1761

Mistra Battery is one of the largest coastal batteries to be found in the Maltese islands. It consists of a roughly circular gun platform with a low parapet en barbette, a shallow ditch, and two large blockhouses with a central redan, all fitted with musketry loopholes closing off the rear. The battery originally had a parapet with three embrasures facing the seaward side of the bay, which parapet has now been rebuilt. The battery was one of the first to

be built in 1714 but continued to be developed during Grand Master Pinto's reign, as evidenced by his coat of arms above the entranceway.

ST ANTHONY BATTERY, GOZO

Map 1 – P4
1732

St Anthony Battery, built at Ras il-Qala, Gozo in 1732, is unique for its polygonal plan and the fact that it survives in a largely unadulterated setting. It appears to have been designed by the Order's resident military engineer, Charles Francois de Mondion. It is built of hardstone quarried from the vicinity. Its main defensive features are its parapet with 11 embrasures, a centrally mounted blockhouse (reconstructed),

and a musketry wall with a central redan closing off the gorge, designed to protect the landward approaches.

ST JULIAN'S BATTERY, TAS-SLIEMA

Map 1 – K8
1715

The first mention of a battery at St Julian's Bay is found in 1714, when Commander Mongontier set aside the sum of 166 scudi for the construction of a battery on the seaward side of St Julian's Tower. By 1716 a total of 587 scudi had been disbursed on its construction. By this stage the work had acquired a semicircular platform and four embrasures on its seaward side and a musketry wall with a redan

and ditch on its landward side. In 1770 this battery was armed with four 18-pdr iron guns. These were reduced to three in 1785.

Above right: Remains of the rock-hewn moat of San Petronio Battery, built at the tip of Gallows Point (present-day Ricasoli Point) in 1602 to prevent slaves from escaping the harbour. In 1629, a tower (known as Orsi Tower) was added to the battery as shown in Willem Schellinks' drawing (above left). Both tower and battery were destroyed by a storm in 1821.

Top row, left to right: Ferretti/Qajjenza Battery; Għżira Battery, Birżebbuġa; Riħama Battery, St Thomas Bay, Marsaskala. Below: St Mary Battery, Comino. Bottom: Left: Vendôme Battery, Armier. Right: L-Aħrax Battery and Tower, l/o Mellieħa.

REDOUBTS

Apart from the coastal batteries, the island-wide system of coastal defence adopted by the Knights in the eighteenth century relied on another important component, the redoubt.

Unlike the batteries, however, which were usually sited at the mouth of the bays and designed to engage enemy ships and boats with their cannon, the redoubts were intended

to serve as infantry strongpoints against landed troops and prevent them from setting up beachheads. In shape and form there was little to distinguish these redoubts from the coastal batteries, other than the fact that these usually lacked embrasures for cannon. The majority of redoubts in Malta and Gozo were built to a more or less pentagonal plan. These were enclosed by shallow parapets, fitted with a single blockhouse at the gorge and surrounded by shallow ditches. Eleven redoubts were built following this standard pattern. The second category, of which only a handful were built, were tower-like in form (known as *tour-reduits*), with walls pierced with numerous musketry loopholes. The only surviving example of this kind can be found in Marsaxlokk Bay.

Left: St George's Redoubt, Birżebbuġa.

1. Blockhouse
2. Doorway to platform
3. High wall closing off gorge and flanks of redoubt pierced with musketry loopholes
4. Infantry parapet with banquette
5. Interior with arches
6. Vaulted interior
7. Entrance with drawbridge

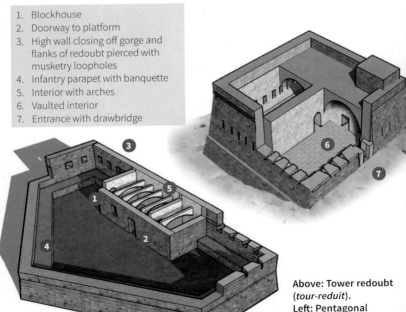

Above: Tower redoubt (*tour-reduit*).
Left: Pentagonal Vendôme-style redoubt.

SALINA RIGHT REDOUBT

Map 1 – G6
1715

Salina Redoubt (Salina Right Redoubt) or, as it was later called, Ximenes Redoubt, is a small structure onto which was added a series of salt magazines intended to store the produce from the nearby salt pans. Originally the redoubt contained a small blockhouse, but this was removed and replaced by a large magazine, while some time after 1741 the redoubt was also fitted with a fougasse which was cut into the bedrock inside the walled enclosure. An escutcheon with the coat of arms of Grand Master

Ximenes crowns the entrance into the smaller of the two magazines, grafted onto the redoubt.

MARSASKALA REDOUBT

Map 1 – N12
1715

Marsaskala Redoubt is a pentagonal-plan redoubt which differs from the standard design by having high walls along the flanks and gorge, all fitted with musketry loopholes and designed to protect its small garrison from the high ground to the rear of the structure. Today the structure also has an entrance on its outer faces, but this is a modern opening. When built in 1715 the redoubt cost the sum

of 868 scudi. It had no permanent armament.

BAHAR IĊ-ĊAGĦAQ REDOUBT

Map 1 – H7
1715

Baħar iċ-Ċagħaq Redoubt, also known as Vendôme Redoubt, was built to the standard pentagonal plan adopted for most of the redoubts built in 1715. It has retained most of its features, although various modern elements were eventually added to it. When built in 1715 it cost the Order's treasury the sum of 913 scudi. The salient of the redoubt was used for defensive purposes during the Second World

War. This redoubt is nowadays used as a catering establishment.

4 VENDÔME REDOUBT, MARSAXLOKK

Map 1 – M14

1715

Also known as Qrajten or Craite Redoubt, this structure on the Marsaxlokk seafront was constructed in the manner of an infantry blockhouse of the *tour-reduit* type. It has a square plan and its sloping walls are perforated with musketry loopholes. Internally the structure is divided into two barrel-vaulted rooms. The roof is enveloped by a thick parapet and the main entrance, which was served by a small drawbridge, is situated on the rear landward side of the structure. When built in 1715–1716 it cost the Order the sum of 1,051 scudi.

5 CREVELLI REDOUBT, ARMIER

Map 1 – C3

1715

Crevelli Redoubt, also known as Armier or Barriera Redoubt, is a typical pentagonal-plan redoubt with a central blockhouse. With its blockhouse recently repaired, it is one of the best surviving examples of this typology of coastal redoubt. The structure is also surrounded by a low ditch. When built in 1715–1716 it cost the Order the sum of 955 scudi. An inscription on the lintel above the main entrance reads:

IL VEN. PRIORE DI CAPUA F. FERDINANDO CREVELLI. This work housed no defensive heavy armament.

6 ESKALAR REDOUBT, ARMIER

Map 1 – C4

1715

Eskalar Redoubt, also known as Hossiliet Redoubt, was a typical pentagonal-plan redoubt with a central blockhouse. However, today it no longer has its blockhouse, and all that survives of the structure is its pentagonal platform and some traces of the low ditch which enveloped it. When built in 1716 Eskalar Redoubt cost the Knights the sum of 1,239 scudi. There are no records to show that the structure was ever armed with cannon.

THE FOUGASSE

The fougasse, or *fogazza a selci*, is one of the most interesting adjuncts of coastal defence employed by the Knights for the defence of the island. This was a kind of rock-hewn mortar, cut into the rocky foreshore and designed to fire large quantities of stone onto approaching enemy ships. In all, some 50 fougasses were built in Malta, with another 14 in Gozo. Of these only a handful have survived, and the best examples can be seen at Salina Bay, Madliena, and Ramla Bay in Gozo.

Although the first mention of the fougasse is encountered in around 1715, these defensive elements were only introduced to Malta in the course of 1741, according to the design of the resident engineer, Francesco Marandon.

Marandon fired his first experimental *fogazza a selci* on 28 September 1740, and this prototype can still be seen on the rocky foreshore beneath English Curtain in Valletta. On the day of its

Above: Madliena fougasse and tower.
Bottom: Cutaway drawing showing an armed fougasse primed and ready to be fired at approaching ships.

baptism of fire, this experimental fougasse was filled with 306 stone boulders of various sizes and fired with a charge of 83 *rotoli* of ordinary gunpowder. It is said to have propelled the said mass of stone over a distance of some 300 m, raising it, in the process, to a maximum height of 60 to 80 m.

ENTRENCHMENTS

One of the fortification elements that was to characterize the eighteenth century was the result of the Hospitallers' efforts to ring off the shores of the Maltese islands with a continuous line of walls, in an attempt to transform the islands, literally, into a veritable fortress. This defensive strategy depended upon the construction of an unbroken line of trinceri (or trinceramenti).

These bastioned seawalls, fitted with their own rock-hewn ditches, were designed to present a physical barrier to invasion. In practice, this strategy involved the construction of many miles of fortifications, and the implementation of this very ambitious scheme, as a result, soon ran into very serious difficulties. Consequently, only a small portion of the coastline was fitted out in the manner envisaged by the Order's military engineers.

Among the surviving entrenchments that were actually constructed and can still be seen today are those at Birżebbuġa, Spinola, Armier, Ta' Qassisu (Mellieħa), iż-Żewwieq (Gozo) and Għajn Tuffieħa. Many of these coastal entrenchments were built to the formal conventions of

Underwater wall, Ramla Bay, Gozo.

the bastioned trace, while others were constructed in a much cheaper and ephemeral manner such as rubble walls in the pietra a secco manner.

The emergency measures of 1761, triggered off by the episode of the mutiny and conquest of the Turkish ship Corona Ottomana, when the Maltese feared a retaliatory attack by the Turks, saw what was effectively the last serious effort in the construction of these massive coastal defences. Many of the works were actually abandoned halfway through after nearly a decade of construction, largely because the money had run out and also because the Knights began to realize that the notion of an island-wide defensive scheme, involving endless miles of ramparts, was then far beyond the Order's logistical and military capabilities.

1 ARMIER ENTRENCHMENT, MELLIEĦA

Map 1 – C4–D3

1761

2 | **TA' QASSISU ENTRENCHMENT, MELLIEHA BAY**

Map 1 – C4

1761

3 | **TARĠA GAP ENTRENCHMENT, NAXXAR**

Map 1 – G8–H8

1722

4 | **SPINOLA ENTRENCHMENT, ST JULIAN'S**

Map 1 – J8–K9

1761

BRITISH FORTIFICATIONS

MODIFICATIONS TO HOSPITALLER FORTS

On gaining possession of Malta, the British military found itself occupying one of the most formidable fortresses in the Mediterranean. The first reaction was to survey the vast extent of fortifications and rationalize the defence.

Particular attention was given to the rearrangement of the artillery. As the years wore on and the technology of warfare began to change, it also became necessary not only to update the defensive armaments but also to adapt the old fortified works to new requirements. Very often this involved the redesigning and partial rebuilding of areas of various sections of fortifications. At times, proposals were even considered for the total demolition of some forts, with a view to replacing them with new modern defences, but these initiatives were never implemented.

The most notable changes began to take place in the late 1850s and 1860s, when the fortifications, particularly those required for coastal defence, began to receive the heavy RML guns and their magazines. In places, these massive cannon required new casemated emplacements, protected by armoured shields, and these, in turn, required a massive overhaul of many of the bastions, particularly at Fort St Elmo and Fort Ricasoli. In the twentieth century many of these emplacements were once again changed and rebuilt in concrete to take more modern breech-loading guns, their shell and cartridge stores, and searchlights.

Previous page: Fort Madalena dominating the heights overlooking the northeastern coast with Qalet Marku Tower in the distance.
Top: Abercrombie Bastion.
Below: Fort St Elmo and the Carafa enceinte – more commonly referred to by the British military as 'Lower St Elmo'.

FORT ST ELMO
VALLETTA
Map 1 – L10

The British refortification of Fort St Elmo and the surrounding Carafa enceinte, which came to be known as Lower St Elmo, began very early in the course of the 19th century. The first British alterations involved the erection of a continuous wall with musketry loopholes running along the whole length of the land front of the fort. This was followed by a remodelling of the flank and left face of St Gregory Bastion, which was fitted with a guardhouse and a casemated battery as well as a sally port fitted with a box-machicolation opening down by the shore. The 1860s then saw a major redesign and rebuilding programme of the main bastioned seafront, as the three main bastions of St Gregory, Conception (renamed Ball's Bastion) and St John (renamed Abercrombie Bastion) were refitted with powerful casemated batteries equipped with their underground shell and cartridge magazines for heavy RML coastal guns.

By the 1880s these guns were considered obsolete and the Carafa enceinte was remodelled to take the more modern breech-loading guns mounted on concrete barbette emplacements. The cavalier of the fort

Above: Parapet with musketry loopholes and gun embrasure on the salient of the right demi-bastion on the land front. Below: Concrete Harbour Command Post situated on top of the cavalier.

also underwent a series of alterations to accommodate a succession of guns, beginning with a battery for RML guns followed by a concrete emplacement for a 10-inch BL gun on a disappearing hydropneumatic carriage.

The last phase, prior to the Second World War, saw the replacement of

the barbette-mounted BL guns with Quick-firing (QF) guns mounted in metal turrets and fitted with concrete fire control towers. Five such turrets, each mounting twin 6-pdr guns, were positioned along the Carafa enceinte, starting from St Lazarus Bastion and terminating at St Gregory Bastion. The cavalier was also reshaped, filled in with concrete and converted into a harbour command post.

The ramparts of the Carafa enceinte were also fitted with a series of searchlight emplacements (called Defence Electric Lights or DEL and later Coastal Artillery Search Lights or CASL). At the turn of the century a breakwater was built just outside the enceinte, protecting the harbour entrance, and this element, particularly its metal viaduct, was to feature prominently during the Italian E-boat attack on the Grand Harbour in July 1941. The QF guns around Fort St Elmo were instrumental in defeating the Italian attack.

Top to bottom: Concrete Fire Control Tower for twin 6-pdr QF gun emplacement;
Open gorge of casemated battery on Abercrombie Curtain;
Detail of the flank of St Gregory Bastion, with its sally port and machicolation;
Battery on St Gregory Bastion.

FORT MANOEL
MANOEL ISLAND

Map 1 – K9

Fort Manoel underwent few changes under the British military. These were largely restricted to the alterations made to St Anthony Bastion in an attempt to transform this seaward-facing bulwark into a coastal battery. These interventions saw the destruction of one of the two Vauban-style gunpowder magazines and the loss of the original *Gardjola* in 1872, which were swept aside to make way for an emplacement for a 9-inch of 12-ton RML gun mounted en barbette. This was followed, in 1903, with the construction of a battery of three 12-pdr QF guns for in-harbour defence which replaced the old RML gun battery. A small battery of three 6-pdr guns was also erected down by the shore outside the *couvre porte*. Two other emplacements for 12-pdr QF guns were also erected on the covertway facing Tas-Sliema.

A metal bridge was built on the landward side of the fort in 1898. This was designed to span the ditch and provide a landward access into the fort which up until then could only be entered from its seafront gate facing Valletta.

Fort Manoel was heavily damaged during the Second World War when, as a result of enemy aerial bombing, it lost a large section of the casemated cavalier curtain and a considerable section of the church of St Anthony of Padua. Both these elements have been reconstructed in the course of restoration works.

Top and below: Glacis and ditch of Fort Manoel with HAA gun emplacement.
Above: The 12-pdr QF battery on St Anthony Bastion.
Below left: 3-gun QF battery outside the sea curtain.

3 FORT RICASOLI
KALKARA

Map 1 – L10

Fort Ricasoli, like Fort St Elmo, was considered as one of the most important works of fortification by the British military because of its position at the entrance to the Grand Harbour. As such it received special attention and underwent a continual process of rearmament and refortification throughout most of the 19th and early 20th centuries. The 1860s, in particular, saw a major rebuilding of the main bastioned seafront, which was refitted with powerful casemated batteries equipped with their underground shell and cartridge magazines for heavy RML coastal guns.

By the 1880s these guns were replaced with concrete barbette emplacements for BL guns. The last phase, prior to the Second World War, saw the replacement of the barbette mounted BL guns with Quick-firing (QF) guns mounted in metal turrets and fitted with concrete fire control towers. The fort had various other structures added to it, such as vaulted caponiers in the ditch, an internal entrenchment (which stood behind No. 4 Bastion, now no longer standing) and two gunpowder magazines. Fort Ricasoli also lost

Top: Aerial view of the gun emplacements facing the entrance to the Grand Harbour.
Above: Detail of scarp musketry gallery situated in the ditch.
Below: Armoured embrasures of the casemated battery situated in the curtain near No. 4 Bastion as seen from the open sea.

a section of its left demi-bastion when mutineers fired its gunpowder magazine in 1807.

FORT TIGNÉ
TAS-SLIEMA

Map 1 – L9

Fort Tigné suffered considerably at the hands of the British military over the course of the nineteenth and twentieth centuries, as a result of their attempts to adapt the structure to a succession of increasingly heavy guns. The first significant alterations were made in the course of the late 1860s, when its original parapets were remodelled to take six 9-inch of 12-ton RML guns mounted behind armoured shields. By 1885, however, it was being viewed as too weak in relation to the importance of the strategic position that it occupied at the mouth of Marsamxett Harbour, and ideas were even put forward for its demolition in order for it to make way for a larger more heavily armed work of fortification. Fortunately these proposals were abandoned and instead a battery of two 9.2-inch BL guns was erected on the glacis outside the fort in 1901. This was replaced, in 1937, with a new battery for three 6-inch BL guns placed in roofed concrete emplacements. In 1899 a Brennan torpedo station was

Above: One of the three emplacements for the 6-inch BL guns of Tigné Battery (1937).
Below: Original counterscarp musketry gallery converted into gun crew shelter.
Bottom: Concrete aprons of Tigné Battery.

installed on the shoreline beneath the fort in an attempt to provide underwater defence for the harbour entrance.

1 FORT VERDALA

BORMLA (COSPICUA)

Map 3 – L11
1844–1852

Fort Verdala was begun in 1852 and incorporated into the Sta Margherita Lines to serve as stronghold within the vast area of ground enclosed by the Firenzuola and Cottonera enceintes. Fort Verdala was completed in 1856 and by 1886 was armed mainly with 24-pdr smooth-bore howitzers. This armament was removed in the 1890s and thereafter the fort was used as a large barrack complex to accommodate military personnel. After World War II it was used as naval stores.

The main gate of Fort Verdala opening onto Bormla.

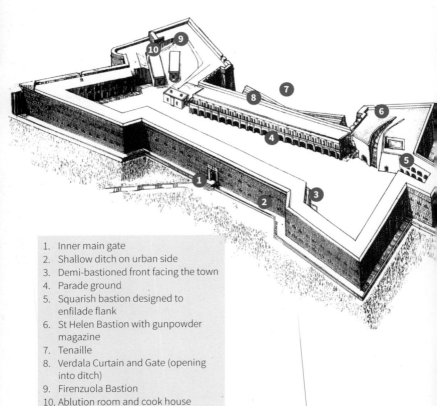

1. Inner main gate
2. Shallow ditch on urban side
3. Demi-bastioned front facing the town
4. Parade ground
5. Squarish bastion designed to enfilade flank
6. St Helen Bastion with gunpowder magazine
7. Tenaille
8. Verdala Curtain and Gate (opening into ditch)
9. Firenzuola Bastion
10. Ablution room and cook house

Above, clockwise from top left: View of the external ramparts; Verdala Gate incorporated into the British fort; *La Dame*, a defensive feature designed to prevent enemy soldiers from moving along the parapet; Internal barracks of Fort Verdala. Below: Aerial view of Fort Verdala showing how the British fort was fitted into the original enceinte of the Sta Margherita (Firenzuola) enceinte. Linked to it is the open gorge of St Clement Retrenchment.

ST CLEMENT RETRENCHMENT
BORMLA (COSPICUA)

Map 3 – L11

1849–1860

Designed to command the high ground overlooking the Grand Harbour, the Cottonera Lines were built by Grand Master Nicolas Cotoner in 1670. Apart from seriously encumbering the Order's financial resources they also proved to be too enormous to be properly manned and defended.

When the British military took over the island's defence, they found themselves burdened with a vast and unfinished defensive work. Moreover, the large unoccupied space between the Cottonera and Sta Margherita Lines could enable an enemy that would have managed to breach the outer lines, to roam around at will and attack the Sta Margherita Lines.

The gorge of the huge bastions of Cottonera Lines were also considered vulnerable to attack from the rear. It was not until the 1840s, however, that the British attempted to solve this problem, revising Bourlamaque's proposal in 1761 for the construction of a hornwork projecting from the Sta Margherita Lines. In 1849 work began on what came to be known as St Clement Retrenchment, a powerful casemated and flanked fort which divided the ground behind the Cottonera enceinte into two areas that could be swept by the batteries of guns.

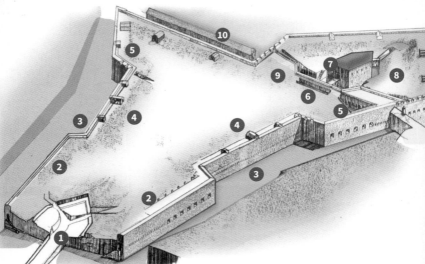

1. Place-of-arms of original covertway incorporated into gorge of retrenchment
2. Casemated demi-bastion with gun embrasures and musketry loopholes
3. Flanking ditch
4. Curtain with musketry loopholes
5. Sunken barracks in right demi-bastion of retrenchment
6. Steps leading down into retrenchment
7. Redoubt
8. St Clement Bastion with expense magazine
9. Demi-bastion
10. Large masonry screen protecting curtain

Above, clockwise from top left: Thick screening wall placed inside the ditch of the Cottonera Lines near St Clement Bastion; St Clement Bastion and Retrenchment; One of the two entrances into St Clement Retrenchment; Aerial view of the blockhouse redoubt with loopholes occupying the retrenchment in St Clement Bastion.
Below: Aerial view of St Clement Retrenchment and the bastioned retrenchment with blockhouse redoubt cut into the gorge of St Clement Bastion. The Verdala School lies within the perimeter of the fort.

3 FORT ST ROCCO

KALKARA

⚜ Map 3 – M10
⧗ 1872, 1900–1905, 1916

Fort St Rocco, begun around 1872 and completed by 1878, originally consisted of a small fort with a fan-shaped plan armed with three 38-ton RML guns with a detached square keep protecting the gorge. Around 1900–1905 a much larger fort was built, obliterating most of the older work, particularly the keep.

Its new armament consisted of three 9.2-inch Mk X BL guns mounted en barbette. Part of the original land front of the old fort was retained. The rear was protected only by a barbed wire fence. At the gorge of the gun emplacement was a large earthen parados on which stood the battery command post. In 1916 the land front was thrust outwards to allow more space for greater barrack accommodation, built to house three officers and 126 men. By the outbreak of the Second World War, Fort St Rocco had been rearmed with three 6-inch BL guns and formed part of the Outer Fire Command of Malta.

General layout of original fort in 1872

1. Square keep
2. Caponier
3. Main entrance
4. Caponier linking keep to battery
5. Ditch
6. Barbette emplacement for 12.5-inch RML gun
7. Magazine building serving as a bonnet
8. Counterscarp gallery
9. Ditch

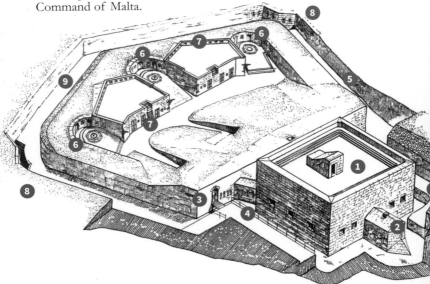

FORT SAN LEONARDO
ŻONQOR, MARSASKALA

 Map 3 – N11
1875–1878

Fort San Leonardo was completed around 1878 and fitted with four 11-inch RML guns. In plan it was a diamond-shaped work with its salient facing inland and occupied by a keep. This was isolated from the main body of the work by an internal ditch flanked by two caponiers.

The whole fort was surrounded by a vertical ditch enfiladed by two single-storey counterscarp galleries with a third demi-caponier situated roughly half way along the ditch. The four guns were arranged asymmetrically on the north side of the seafront. In 1897 the fort was rearmed with two 9.2-inch BL Mark IX guns. The guns were mounted to the right of the four RML gun emplacements. The old RML guns were removed and thrown into the

ditch, where they remained until the 1970s. On the seashore, well below the fort, defence electric lights, housed in tower-like masonry emplacements, provided the fortress guns with the necessary illumination for nocturnal target identification.

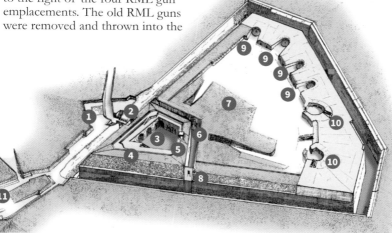

1. Redan (or place-of-arms)
2. Guthrie rolling bridge and main gate
3. Courtyard of casemated keep
4. Field gun emplacements with ramp
5. Battery Command Post for 9.2-inch guns
6. Internal ditch separating keep from main body of the work
7. Glacis within fort
8. Caponier enfilading internal ditch
9. Gun emplacements for four 11-inch of 25-ton RML guns
10. Emplacement for 9.2-inch BL Mk X guns
11. Fleche

Aerial view of Fort San Leonardo. Traces of the Hospitaller 18th-century coastal entrenchment are visible along the length of the rocky shoreline.

Aerial view of Fort St Rocco showing the ditch of the original 1872 battery. The last guns to be mounted inside the forts were three 5.25-inch BL guns placed in new concrete emplacments.

5

FORT ST LUCIAN

MARSAXLOKK

Map 3 – M14

1872–1878

The origins of Fort St Lucian date back to the early seventeenth century, when a large coastal tower was built at Marsaxlokk by Grand Master Wignacourt in 1610. St Lucian Tower, as it was called, remained the focal point of the coastal defences of Marsaxlokk Bay throughout the rest of the Order's stay on the island. In 1715–1716 the tower was fitted with a strong, seaward facing battery and later, in 1795, both tower and battery were enclosed by a ditch and the whole complex rechristened Fort Rohan.

St Lucian Tower was retained by the British military, and in 1874 work began on its enlargement. The new perimeter contained three large casemated gun positions and was constructed in masonry with armoured embrasures for three 10-inch of 18-ton RML guns, and

below them were installed their magazines. On each side of the casemated front were two pits for 64-pdr RML guns on Moncrieff disappearing carriages. Two similar pits for disappearing guns were installed on the rear part of the fort, and designed mainly for land defence.

1. Main entrance into fort served with drawbridge
2. Gun emplacement for 64-pdr RML gun mounted on Moncrieff disappearing carriage (x4)
3. St Lucian Tower (1610) incorporated into the enceinte of the battery to serve as a keep
4. Defensive blockhouse
5. Cutaway showing battery for three 10-inch of 18-ton RML guns
6. Caponiers inside ditch (x4)
7. Parapet
8. Ditch
9. Gateway leading to casemated battery
10. Raised stepped infantry banquette

Left: Aerial view of Fort St Lucian.
Above: Gate originally served by a drawbridge.
Above right: View of the casemated battery as seen from the sea.
Right: Detail of one of the three armoured embrasures for 10-inch RML guns.

6 FORT BINĠEMMA

BINĠEMMA

Map 3 – D9

1875

The first fort to be built on the North-West Front, proposed in 1872 and approved by the Defence Committee in 1873, was Fort Binġemma. Work on the fort began in 1875 and was completed three years later. An irregular-shaped work, Fort Binġemma's design exploited the escarpment of the great fault, where the cliff face provided a natural defence while on the landward side a vertical ditch and a wide parapet isolated the work and established the main defensive perimeter. Flanking defences and enfilading fire were provided by closely spaced scarp and counterscarp galleries, linked by tunnel passages to the keep.

Basically, Fort Binġemma consists of two parts: a main enclosure for the gun emplacements and their magazines, and a diamond-shaped keep. Since the guns and their magazines consumed most of the main enclosure, barrack accommodation was provided within the keep, built of two concentric parts. Entrance into the keep from outside was provided through a counterpoise drawbridge.

Below: Aerial view of concentric diamond-shaped keep of Fort Binġemma.
Bottom: View of the parapet and rock-hewn ditch of Fort Binġemma.
Opposite, bottom: View of the northern cliff face with its gun emplacements.

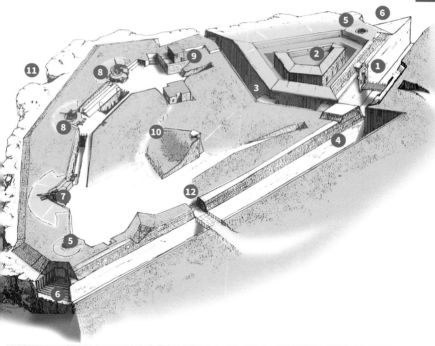

General layout of Fort Binġemma c. 1930

1. Main entrance into fort served with drawbridge
2. Concentric keep
3. Ditch separating keep from main body of fort protected by three caponiers
4. Ditch
5. Gun emplacement for 64-pdr RML gun mounted on Moncrieff disappearing carriage (x2)
6. Embrasure for casemated gun emplacement (x2)
7. Barbette emplacement for 9.2-inch BL gun
8. Barbette emplacement for 6-inch BL gun (x2)
9. Battery Command Post for 6-inch guns
10. Battery Command Post for 9.2-inch gun
11. Cliff face
12. Cutting in parapet with gateway

7 FORT SLIEMA

TAS-SLIEMA

Map 3 – C6–D6

1872

Fort Sliema, later better known as Sliema Point Battery, was one of the four coastal works projected by Colonel Jervois in 1866 and appears to have been directly inspired by him, since its design reflects a certain Gothic character – with its decorated cornice, carved loopholes and embrasures, and moulded archway – which was also a feature of his earlier forts on Alderney. Such features gave the work the appearance more of a medieval castle than a heavy-gun fort.

Work on Fort Sliema, which was sited on the rocky shoreline north of Fort Tigné, began in 1872. The fort was originally intended to mount two 23-ton guns but by June of 1872, while the fort was still under construction, the Defence Committee decided to improve its armament to four guns. These were two 11-inch of 25-ton RML

Above: The land front of Fort Sliema, with its observation tower.
Bottom: View of the main entrance bridge, and hexagonal keep of Fort Sliema. The gate was originally served by a Guthrie rolling drawbridge.

guns and two 10-inch of 18-ton RML guns, all inside casemates and behind iron shields.

In January of 1873 there was a further amendment, when it was recommended that the two 11-inch guns be replaced by two 12.5-inch of 38-ton RML guns. These were eventually installed, in 1878, behind armoured fronts and on rotating platforms.

Right: Two views of the casemated emplacements and armoured shields on the seaward-facing side of the fort.

General layout of Fort Sliema as it would have stood around 1880

1. Main entrance into fort
2. Guthrie rolling bridge
3. Ditch
4. Casemated keep
5. Casemated emplacement with armoured embrasure for 10-inch of 18-ton RML gun (x2)
6. Casemated emplacement with rotating platform and armoured front for 12.5-inch of 38-ton RML gun (x2)
7. Caponier with musketry loopholes (x2) (buried)
8. Parade ground
9. Spur

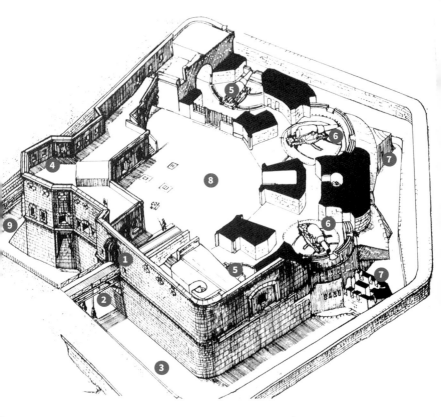

8 FORT MADALENA

MADLIENA

Map 3 – 18
1878–1881

The second fort to be built on the North-West Front during the 1870s was Fort Madalena. Its position necessitated that it serves a dual land/coastal defence role, a purpose which was eventually modified and restricted only to coastal defence, particularly during the last phase in its history.

Work on Fort Madalena began in June 1878 and was completed by 1881 at a cost of £9,400. Originally the fort consisted of a symmetrical pentagonal plan with its salient angle facing inland. The work, which was built on the site of an old chapel, was surrounded by a narrow and vertical ditch, where flanking defences were provided by means of four two-storey counterscarp galleries linked to the fort by means of underground tunnels. There was no keep.

By 1892 the fort's armament came to consist of four 6-inch guns on hydropneumatic mountings, but in 1905 all the guns were removed and two 6-inch BL Mk VII guns were mounted on the north-west corner of the fort, while two 9.2-inch BL guns were mounted in an open earthwork battery just outside the fort.

Top: The main gate into Fort Madalena.
Below: Aerial view of Fort Madalena and its attached 9.2-inch coastal battery.

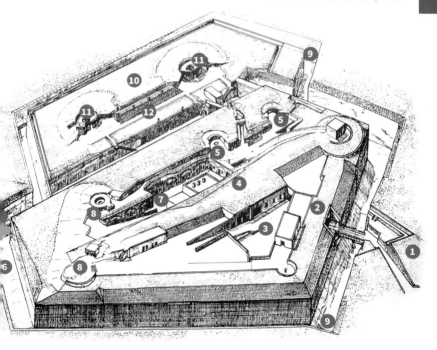

1. Redan with cutting in glacis
2. Main gate with Guthrie rolling bridge
3. Inner courtyard
4. Casemated traverse
5. Emplacement for 6-inch BL gun on HP mounting (x2)
6. Ditch
7. Outer courtyard
8. Barbette emplacement for 6-inch BL gun
9. Counterscarp gallery
10. Battery added in 1905
11. Emplacement for 9.2-inch BL gun
12. Sunken area leading to magazines of 9.2-inch BL gun battery

Above right: View of the exterior slope of the parapet revetted in stone, rock-hewn scarp, and ditch of Fort Madalena.
Right: Aerial view of Fort Madalena showing the 9.2-inch battery grafted onto the seaward front of the original fort.

9 FORT MOSTA

MOSTA

Map 3 – G8

1878–1880

Occupying a central position along the escarpment of the Great Fault, Fort Mosta (or Fort Musta as was its official British designation) was the most strategically placed land fort on the Victoria Lines. Originally designed as one of three isolated strongholds on the North-West Front, the proposal for the construction of Fort Mosta was approved in 1873. The first of the three forts to be initiated was Fort Binġemma, begun in 1875, followed by Fort Madalena in 1878. By the time of General Simmons' visit to Malta in February 1878 (who later became Governor of Malta), work on Fort Mosta had not yet commenced. Begun later in 1878, Fort Mosta is a typical example of a British hill fort, consisting of two main component parts: a polygonal enceinte and a focal casemated keep, pentagonal in plan. The fort occupies the cliff faces on the spur of land at the mouth of Wied il-Għasel and was built, apparently according to available documentation and some archaeological evidence, on the site of a Bronze Age citadel (De Grognet). Catacombs dating to the fourth or fifth century AD were found under the fort and they still exist.

1. Main gate into casemated keep with Guthrie rolling bridge
2. Courtyard of keep
3. Platform for field gun
4. Ditch
5. Vaulted embrasures in keep
6. Covered way on outer battery
7. Counterscarp gallery (x3)
8. Earthen parados
9. Emplacement for 6-inch BL gun on HP disappearing mount (x2)
10. Shell and cartridge stores
11. Two haxo-style casemates for 64-pdr guns on traversing carriages
12. Masonry buttresses

Above: Aerial view of Fort Mosta showing its two main components – the pentagonal keep and the large external battery.
Right: View of the keep of Fort Mosta seen from Naxxar.
Below: Aerial view showing the gorge of the keep of Fort Mosta with its gateway and bridge spanning the ditch, originally served by a Guthrie rolling bridge.

10 FORT PEMBROKE

PEMBROKE

Map 3 – J8
1875–1878

Fort Pembroke was completed in 1879 and like the other British forts built during this period, its design followed the conventions of the polygonal system of fortification. In plan it consisted of an elongated hexagon surrounded with a continuous vertical ditch flanked by three two-storey counterscarp galleries, protected by their own shallow ditch and iron fence and armed with carronades. Internally, the enclosure was occupied by the gun emplacements which, being in the main three barbette positions separated by traverses, were installed on the sea-facing ramparts. A large casemated traverse, running from north to south, roughly bisected the internal area into two equal halves. The casemates provided accommodation for a garrison of seventy-one rank and file. Fort Pembroke was one of the few British forts in Malta to include an elaborate covertway. By the end of the 19th century the role of Fort Pembroke as a defensive coastal position was taken over by a new battery erected in the vicinity of the fort and armed with two 9.2-inch BL guns.

General layout of Fort Pembroke as it would have stood around 1878

1. Redan with cutting in glacis
2. Main gate with Guthrie rolling bridge
3. Short stretch of covertway with traverse
4. Parapet with traverse
5. Fleche with platforms for fieldguns
6. Courtyard
7. Large casemated traverse
8. Barbette emplacement for 11-inch of 25-ton RML gun (x3)
9. Counterscarp gallery
10. Gun emplacement for 64-pdr RML gun mounted on Moncrieff disappearing carriage
11. Ditch

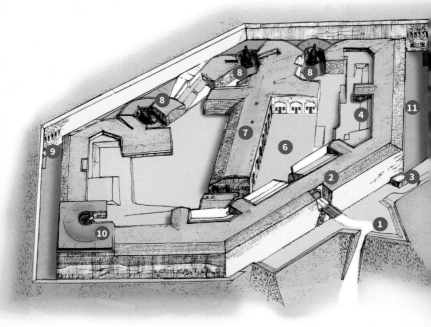

Above: Aerial view of Fort
Pembroke, showing its
hexagonal design.
Right: Emplacement for 11-inch
of 25-ton RML gun mounted on
en barbette with sunken way for
loading gun crew and shield by
earthen traverses.
Bottom right: One of the three
two-tiered counterscarp galleries
showing its musketry loopholes
and embrasures for carronades.

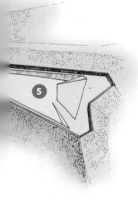

Aerial view of the seaward-facing front of Fort Pembroke.

View of the rock-hewn communication tunnels leading to the counterscarp galleries around the perimeter of the fort.

11 FORT DELIMARA

DELIMARA

Map 3 – N15
1876–1878

Work on Fort Delimara began in January 1876 and was eventually completed by 1878. It was designed to command the entrance into Marsaxlokk harbour and as such was sited at the tip of the Delimara peninsula. Initially its armament consisted of six 38-ton guns protected in casemates by iron shields and firing from the cliff face. Flanking defences were provided by three counterscarp galleries armed with eight 32-pdr smooth-bore breech loading guns. A steel palisade lined the counterscarp and helped guard against a direct infantry assault.

A new armament of one 9.2-inch on disappearing mount and two 6-inch BL guns was installed in 1892, but by 1910 this was once again changed to two 9.2-inch BL guns. Some of the 12.5-inch of 38-ton wrought-iron rifled muzzle-loading guns are still to be found *in situ*, mounted on their original traversing carriages inside the casemates.

General layout showing Fort Delimara as it would have stood around 1890

1. Main gate with Guthrie rolling bridge
2. Barbette emplacement for 12.5-inch of 38-ton RML gun
3. Counterscarp gallery
4. Barrack accommodation
5. Traverse-cum-expense magazine
6. Parados
7. Barbette emplacement for 9.2-inch BL gun (x2)
8. Covered communication passage
9. Casemated emplacement with armoured embrasure for 12.5-inch of 38-ton RML gun (x6)
10. Ditch

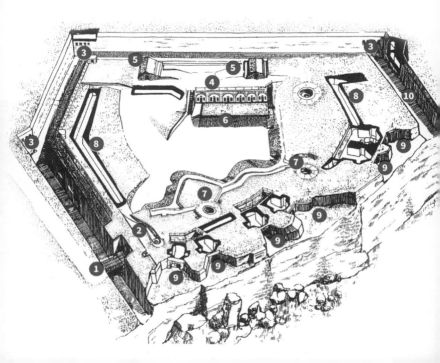

Above: Aerial view of Fort Delimara showing the casemated gun emplacements crowning the cliff face overlooking Marsaxlokk Harbour.

Left: One of the six 12.5-inch of 38 tons RML guns which once protected the entrance to Marsaxlokk harbour, still to be found *in situ* inside its vaulted casemate.

Below: Aerial view of a section of the interior area and the landward perimeter of Fort Delimara, showing the infantry parapet pierced with rifle loopholes which runs along the superior slope of the original earthen parapet.

12 FORT TAS-SILĠ

MARSAXLOKK

Map 3 – N14

1879–1883

Fort Tas-Silġ occupied the highest part of the Delimara promontory and was designed to act as an infantry keep for the whole position. The original proposed armament of twelve 64-pdr 7-inch guns on wrought-iron dwarf platforms was modified, in 1882, to six 64-pdr RML guns on permanent disappearing carriages, three 40-pdr RBL on overbank siege travelling carriages together with six smooth-bore BL guns for flank defence. The latter were to be placed inside the three bulbous caponiers enfilading the ditch of the fort.

None of the guns had been installed by 1884, for although the fort partook of the character of a coast defence work, there was no particular part of the coast which it was suited to resist an attack from. Owing to its ambiguous role, Fort Tas-Silġ did not continue to feature among those fortifications required for coastal defence, and consequently never received any new breech-loading guns.

By 1903 it was no longer required for defence, and was relegated to use as an army depot and wireless station, a role it continued to fulfil right down to the 1960s.

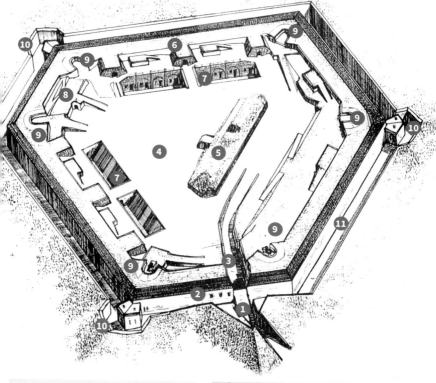

1. Redan with cutting in glacis
2. Main gate with Guthrie rolling bridge
3. Casemates opening onto three armoured embrasures
4. Parade ground
5. Parados
6. Traverse-cum-expense magazine
7. Sunken courtyard opening into barrack accommodation
8. Platform for field artillery
9. Barbette emplacement for 64-pdr RML gun mounted (x6)
10. Caponier (x3)
11. Ditch

Left: Aerial view of Fort Tas-Silġ.
Right: The ditch of Fort Tas-Silġ was defended by three bulbous caponiers.

13 FORT BENGHISA

BIRŻEBBUĠA

Map 3 – M16

1910–1912

Fort Benghisa represents the last of the major coastal defence forts built by the British in the polygonal style of fortification. Indeed it was the last fort – in the conventional sense of the word, with ditch, parapet, and counterscarp galleries – to be built in Malta. The original project dates to May 1909, when British engineers designed a closed work for two 9.2-inch BL guns, and was to be built in the vicinity of Għar Ħasan. The original plan was eventually redesigned to include a larger perimeter, and by 1912 the new work, called Fort Benghisa, was given an armament of two 9.2-inch Mk X BL guns and two 6-inch Mk VII BL guns mounted en barbette and separated from one another by underground magazines. In 1938 the two 6-inch BL guns were dismantled and after the war, during the 1950s, the 9.2-inch guns were also removed and their emplacements were concreted in, while three new gun emplacements were constructed to take three 5.25-inch HA/LA dual-purpose guns.

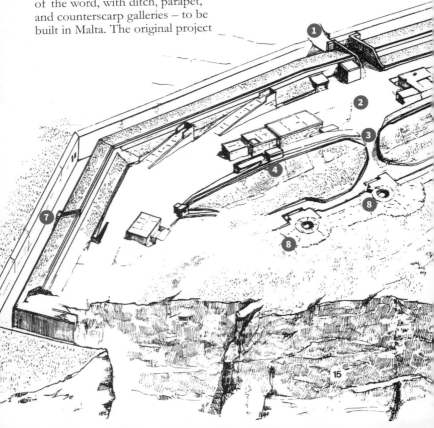

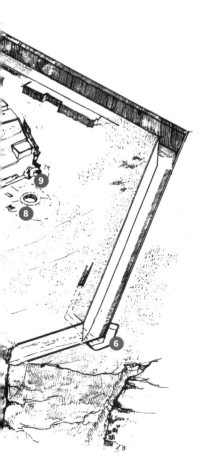

Aerial views of the fort. The southern part of the enceinte is unfortified as it forms part of the cliff face.

General layout of Fort Bengħisa showing the various gun emplacements

1. Main gate
2. Parade ground
3. Cutting in parados
4. Battery command post for 9.2-inch guns situated on parados
5. Battery command post for 6-inch guns situated on parados
6. Counterscarp gallery
7. Ditch
8. Emplacement for 5.25-inch BL gun (x3)
9. Emplacement for 9.2-inch BL gun (x2)

14 FORT CAMPBELL

SELMUN

🏛 Map 3 – E5
⧗ 1937–1938

Fort Campbell was built in 1937/1938, prior to the outbreak of the war, and was designed to serve as an examination battery challenging ships approaching the Grand Harbour from the North. The most striking feature of Fort Campbell was its informal plan designed to imitate the pattern of the adjoining terraced fields. Perimeter defence was provided by a number of machine-gun posts, or bunkers, placed at irregular intervals along the line of defence, particularly where the enceinte changed direction, and in other places by a few rifle loopholes.

Internally, the enclosure was occupied by a small number of buildings. Much care was taken to scatter all the main component parts of the fort – the command post, gun emplacements, water tank, direction posts and barrack accommodation and magazines – across the whole area, to form a system of dispersed points, in order not to create any concentration of buildings which would stand out quite clearly when seen from the air. Two 6-inch BL coastal guns, mounted in concrete emplacements, provided the fort's armament, though a third was added later on.

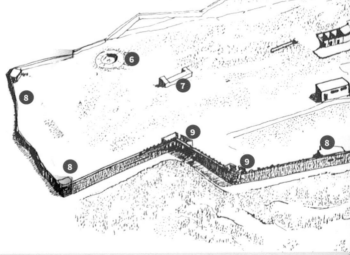

1. Main gate
2. External barracks
3. Administrative block and workshops
4. Gun emplacement for 6-inch BL gun on 45 degree mounting with adjoining underground magazines and gun crew shelters (x2)
5. Battery command post
6. No. 3 gun emplacement
7. Gun crew shelter
8. Perimeter defence post BL gun (x6)
9. Rifle loopholes
10. Direction post
11. Operational barrack block for 20 men
12. Underground radar engine room

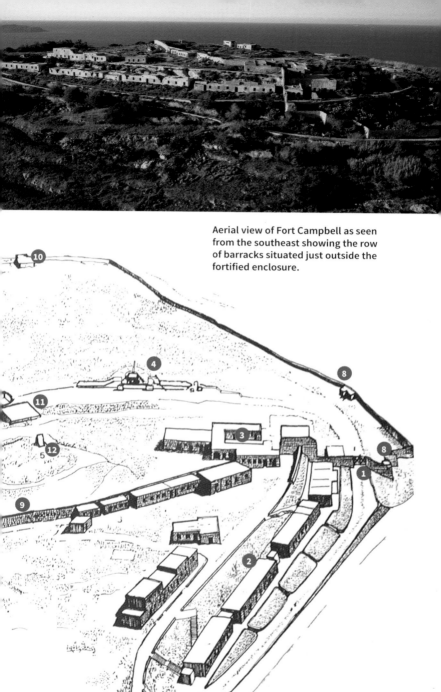

Aerial view of Fort Campbell as seen from the southeast showing the row of barracks situated just outside the fortified enclosure.

Above: Aerial view of Fort Campbell and its surrounding rural landscape. The irregular perimeter wall surrounding the fort was intended to make it hard to spot and distinguish from the air. To the north, on the adjoining plateau, sit the remains of Għajn Ħadid Tower, the first of the coastal towers built by Grand Master de Redin in 1658, and demolished by an earthquake in the mid-nineteenth century.

Left: Aerial view of one of the 6-inch BL gun emplacements with its concrete apron and adjoining roofed loading area.

Right: Aerial view of the ruins of the fort's command centre.
Bottom right: Perimeter defence post camouflaged with rubble stone cladding designed to mimic the surrounding field walls.
Below: Aerial view of the landward-facing perimeter of the fort.

15 MELLIEĦA CIVIL DEFENCE DEPOT

MELLIEĦA

Map 3 – C6

Mellieħa Civil Defence Depot, or Fort Mellieħa as it was also known, is a simple fortified enclosure located in the village of Mellieħa. The compound contains various buildings and structures, including a towering observation post. The perimeter was defended with a handful of machine-gun posts consisting of low covered positions placed on the roofs of buildings.

This military compound was occupied by the Civil Defence Corps in the 1950s and 1960s and then by the Armed Forces of Malta in the 1970s. Currently the walled compound serves as the headquarters for the Mellieħa Boys Scout group.

Top: An observation post at Fort Mellieħa.
Right and below: Two aerial views showing the location of the walled enclosure and the layout of its defensible perimeter.

SOUND LOCATOR EMPLACEMENTS

An important adjunct of the anti-aircraft defences was the sound locators. These devices, which pre-dated the radar, were used as a means of detecting incoming unseen enemy aircraft by amplifying the sound of their engines, particularly at night, thereby enabling predictions of probable course and approximate height of the attacking enemy aircraft to allow barrage line of fire to be selected.

These primitive-looking trumpet-like devices with their paraboloid sound receivers were mounted on wheeled chassis and protected within defensible rectangular stone enclosures. A number of such sound locator emplacements can be found scattered around Malta. Structurally, these emplacements consist of a rectangular enclosure of blast walls having a peculiar slightly concave outer slope. A small rectangular shed, which also served as the entrance to the enclosure, was used to shelter the sound locators when not in use. Rifle loopholes, served by concrete firing steps, allowed the crews working the equipment to defend the position.

Top: A camouflaged sound locator during WWII.
Above: Ta' Falka, l/o Dwejra, Malta.
Below: Għajn Tuffieħa.
Bottom: Delle Grazie Battery, Xgħajra.

DEFENSIVE LINES

CORRADINO LINES

GHAJN DWIELI TO CORRADINO

Map 3 – K11–L11

1871

Among the last areas of ground bordering the Grand Harbour area to receive any form of fortification were the Corradino Heights. This hill, overlooking the southern inner extremity of the Grand Harbour, had long since posed a threat to the security of the harbour, mainly because it enabled enemy batteries established there to attack both ships lying at anchor as well as the fortifications of Floriana, Valletta and Senglea.

British plans to fortify the hill appeared as early as 1805, when Captain Dickens RE proposed to occupy the heights with four large redoubts set out over a large quadrilateral of enfiladed ditches. Nothing came of this proposal and in 1851 the problem was raised once again, this time by Lt Col. Emmett CRE, who proposed erecting a strong squarish tower on the hill. Again the project failed to materialize, and it was not until 1871 that the British military began to seal off the area with a continuous line of ramparts which came to be known as the Corradino Lines.

This work of fortification consisted of a fortified enceinte and ditch spanning from the west face of St Paul Bastion on the Cottonera enceinte all the way to Ras Ħanżir. The work was built to the conventions of the polygonal trace and consisted of a long and straight curtain wall flanked with four musketry galleries inside the ditch. The focal point of the enceinte was the salient of the work at the top of the hill, where the British engineers constructed a small battery with two emplacements for 64-pdr guns on Moncrieff disappearing carriages, protected to the rear by a large traverse.

A nineteenth-century photograph showing the Corradino Lines where they descended towards the Grand Harbour and the large gunpowder magazine built by Grand Master Pinto.

Above: View of the two-storey counterscarp gallery protecting the central salient of the fortified enceinte.
Left: Detail of the superior slope of the parapet and platform typical of the ramparts making up most of the Corradino enceinte.

Below: Aerial view of the surviving elements of the Corradino Lines today.

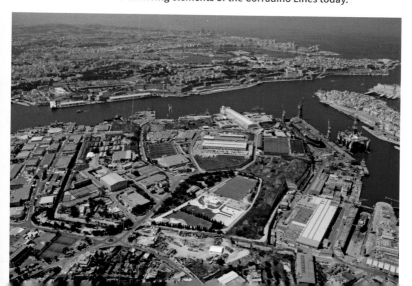

2 DWEJRA LINES
TA' FALKA TO BINĠEMMA

 Map 3 – D9–E9

1881

The Dwejra Lines, begun in 1881 and consisting of a continuous enceinte about one kilometre long, were built to defend an important gap in the North-West Front where the natural defences of the Great Fault did not provide an advantage to the defenders.

The Dwejra Lines consisted of a series of serrated lines of long straight ramparts protected by a parallel ditch and enfiladed by caponiers and scarp galleries, according to the conventions of the polygonal system of fortification. The ramparts are topped by a wide earthen parapet and served by earthen platforms and banquettes. It was originally intended to arm the defensive line with thirty 64-pdr guns mounted en barbette on traversing platforms and siege carriages, but this was soon modified to just five such guns mounted on disappearing carriages plus ten 40-pdr RBL

guns on overbank siege travelling carriages, together with ten 8-inch howitzers and one smooth bore cannon for enfilading fire. None of this armament was ever mounted, however, so in 1899 three emplacements for 5-inch BL guns were built roughly in the centre of the position.

Both extremities of the defensive front, overlooking the valleys, were fortified with musketry parapets. The western extremity facing Binġemma Gap originally had a much longer musketry wall than at present. This was cut down and reshaped during the construction of the Victoria Lines, when it was necessary to link the Dwejra Position to the stop-wall bridging the valley.

In 1900 a defence electric light was installed at the eastern extremity of the Dwejra Lines. The searchlight itself, however, was not approved and was eventually removed. The electric light engine room was situated in a purposely built underground installation to the rear of the emplacement.

Opposite: Musketry parapet overlooking Binġemma Gap after restoration.
Above: The musketry parapet of the stop-wall cutting across the valley at Binġemma Gap.
Right: View of a searchlight emplacement.

Left: One of the scarp-flanking galleries.
Below: View of the stop-wall at Binġemma Gap shown from the inner side as it crosses the valley to link the Dwejra Lines with the infantry wall at ix-Xagħra ta' Binġemma.

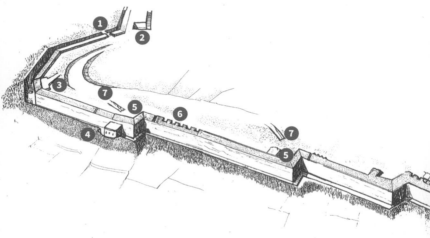

Above: Aerial view of the eastern salient of Dwejra Lines showing its thick earthen parapet and narrow ditch.
Below: A general view of the Dwejra Lines showing its glacis, the largely rock-hewn scarp and earthen superior slope.

Aerial view of the Dwejra enceinte, spanning from Binġemma Gap (right) to Ta' Falka Hill (left). In the background lies Mtarfa with its barracks, and Mdina.

1. Main gate
2. Underground engine room for searchlight
3. Artillery platform for field gun
4. Caponier
5. Scarp flanking gallery
6. Indented parapet for battery of field guns

7. Ramp leading down to scarp gallery
8. Protective emplacements for 64-pdr RML guns on disappearing mounts
9. Battery for three 5-inch BL guns on barbette mountings
10. Searchlight emplacement
11. Sally port leading down into ditch

3 VICTORIA LINES
NORTH-WEST FRONT

Map 3 – B9–I8

1875–1907

Nowhere in the Maltese islands is 'geography' so emphatically exploited for defence than along the line of natural escarpments known as the Great Fault, found north of Mdina. Here, in a fashion reminiscent of Roman lines, the British military erected a complex network of linear fortifications in the latter half of the nineteenth century, to provide a physical barrier to invasion. The reason behind these fortifications was the need to protect the naval installations in the Grand Harbour, then considered so vital for the maintenance of the British fleet, the source of Britain's imperial power in the Mediterranean Sea.

Initially termed the North-West Front, this defensive line consisted of three detached forts (Forts Binġemma, Mosta, and Madalena), an entrenchment (Dwejra Lines),

and a small number of batteries (Targa and San Giovanni) spaced out along the length of the natural escarpment.

By 1897, however, these various strongpoints were considered too detached from one another to provide an effective defence that could seal off the escarpment. As a result it was decided to link all the positions together by means of a continuous masonry wall.

The new defensive front, some 12 km in length, was rebaptized as the 'Victoria Lines', in honour of Queen Victoria's diamond jubilee.

The Victoria Lines, as a result, comprise a unique ensemble of diverse fortified elements brought to form a linear defensive front. The fortified line linking the works together consisted mainly of a rock-hewn escarpment topped by a loopholed parapet wall. In the words of Col. Wood, the defensive

Aerial view of the central elements of the Victoria Lines, with Fort Mosta.

View of the infantry parapet with reconstructed musketry loopholes located in the vicinity of Fort Mosta (visible in the background).

wall rose 'about 6 feet 3 inches high', was built of 'squared stone and the three upper courses' (which included the two courses for the loopholing) were 'set in puzzolana mortar'. A patrol path, to the immediate rear of the parapet, followed the line of the wall along its length. The perimeter was closed off, to its rear, by a low boundary wall which was intended mainly to delineate and mark out the

The stop-wall at Wied il-Faħam, near Madliena.

military property and set it apart from private or public land. The whole defensive line, although built in stone, was conceived largely as a form of fieldwork and had a predominantly organic quality to its layout following, as it did, a sinuous route along the contours of the natural escarpment in an attempt to adapt itself to the lie of the land.

Special attention was given to the fortification of the valleys which cut across the escarpment and created serious gaps in the defensive fronts. Here, the British military engineers constructed defensible causeways, called stop-walls, which crossed over the valley floors and plugged in the approaches up the valleys. Three of these stop-walls are still standing, namely at Binġemma Gap,

Top: The original commemorative marble plaque marking Queen Victoria's Diamond Jubilee in 1897.
Left: Section of the Victoria Lines' parapet wall running along Wied il-Faħam, Madliena.
Below: Concrete emplacements for two QF guns at San Giovanni Battery, overlooking Baħar iċ-Ċagħaq.

Aerial view of the fortified searchlight emplacement at Kunċizzjoni. (Map 3 – C10)

Wied il-Faham (below Madliena) and Wied Anġlu (near Ħal Gharghur). A fourth, and perhaps the most impressive of all the stop-walls, which spanned across Wied il-Ghasel and stood on three large arches, was unfortunately carried away by torrential rain waters in 1979. A small one, at Wied Filep, was eaten away by quarrying activity.

Among the secondary elements that make up the complex network of defences were seven howitzer field batteries, fortified searchlight engine rooms at Kunċizzjoni and Ħal Gharghur, an infantry redoubt at Fomm ir-Riħ, and two munitions depots at Dwejra and Mosta.

Above right: View of the interior of the fortified searchlight emplacement at Kunċizzjoni.
Right: Surviving section of the infantry wall at Ħal Gharghur. (Map 3 – H8)

1

LASCARIS BATTERY

VALLETTA

Map 3 – L10

1854

The British began to build Lascaris Battery in 1854, to provide the Grand Harbour with a defensive battery capable of destroying enemy ships that might succeed in breaking in through the harbour's outer defences. In conjunction with Fort St Angelo, it commanded the inner reaches of the harbour, most importantly the then newly-built dockyard. Lascaris Battery was built in the form of a large masonry, L-shaped double-decker bastion projecting outwards from the flanks of SS Peter and Paul Demi-bastion on the east side of Valletta. It had two rows of casemates on its two faces and flanks which covered nearly all the harbour area. The interior of the bastion was hollow, providing enough space for a

sizable parade yard overlooked by the top floors of casemates. In 1860 the battery was armed with fourteen 8-inch guns, but by 1886 these had been replaced by a 9-inch 12-ton RML gun mounted en barbette in the salient spur and seven

General layout of Lascaris Battery showing its position in relation to the various elements of the Valletta fortifications

1. Main entrance to battery
2. Saluting Battery
3. Upper Barrakka
4. SS Peter and Paul Counterguard
5. Courtyard
6. Roof battery with guns mounted on traversing carriages
7. Rounded projecting shoulder
8. Casemated rampart facing Dockyard Creek
9. Tunnel beneath bastion
10. Casemated rampart facing entrance to harbour with two tiers of gun embrasures

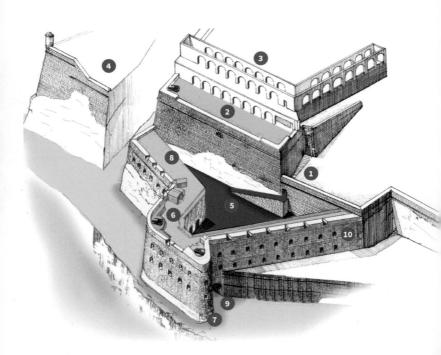

View from across the Grand Harbour showing the manner in which Lascaris Battery was grafted to the flank of the land front enceinte of Valletta. The battery replaced a summer house and garden which had been built by Grand Master Lascaris in the 17th century.

64-pdr mounted inside casemates. Lascaris Battery was disarmed in the 1890s and was eventually used as a naval headquarters. During the Second World War the Combined Operational Headquarters was stationed in Lascaris Bastion, inside underground rock-hewn chambers.

TRYON BATTERY

VALLETTA

🔭 Map 3 – L10
⧗ 1854

A small battery was erected on the rocky foreshore at the foot of St Lazarus Curtain in 1896 to protect the entrance to the Grand Harbour. This work was armed with six 12-pdr QF guns mounted in line on concrete barbette emplacements with covered shelters for gun crews in between. The right side of the battery was protected by three Maxim machine guns while the ammunition magazine was cut into the bedrock of the curtain wall to the rear. A searchlight emplacement

and two observation cells were also cut into the face of the adjoining ramparts. These elements, together with the underground storage facilities and two of the concrete gun emplacements, are the only surviving parts of the battery.

3

CAMBRIDGE BATTERY

TAS-SLIEMA

Map 3 – K9

1878–1886

Cambridge Battery is one of two works of coastal fortification (the other being Rinella Battery) which were purposely built to house and protect the 100-ton Armstrong RML guns sent to Malta for the defence of Valletta and its harbours. Cambridge Battery was erected on a stretch of ground situated between the old Hospitaller Fort Tigné and Fort Sliema (1872) and effectively stood guard over the entrance to Marsamxett Harbour. Of the two batteries, Cambridge Battery was the first to be laid out, with works commencing on 28 August 1878. Although the date on the gate of this battery reads 1880, it was only completed in 1886.

The two 100-ton gun batteries had a quasi-identical layout but for the fact that their plans were inverted, basically forming a mirror image of one another. Still the two designs had some notable differences,

amongst which was the layout of their internal courtyards and the configuration of musketry loopholes and parapets along the gorge of the works.

Cambridge Battery lost both its 100-ton gun (which was cut down and sold as scrap metal) and its three caponiers inside the ditch, but it still retains its counterscarp musketry gallery. The battery also suffered considerable structural damage during WWII but this has since been repaired. It also had its original Guthrie rolling bridge before this was removed and taken to equip another restored fort.

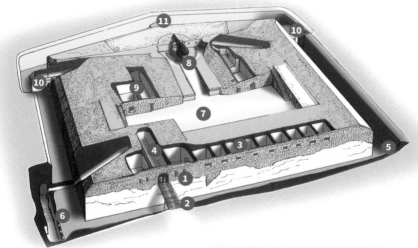

1. Main gate
2. Guthrie rolling bridge
3. Barrack accommodation
4. Entrance passageway with guardrooms
5. Ditch
6. Counterscarp musketry gallery
7. Courtyard
8. 100-ton gun emplacement
9. Cutting showing rooms for accumulator pump and boiler for working traversing and loading mechanism
10. Flanking caponier
11. Salient caponier

Above: Aerial view of the concrete apron and left flank of the battery.
Below: View of the ditch and scarp walls.

4 RINELLA BATTERY
KALKARA
Map 3 – M10
1879–1886

Rinella Battery was the second of the two 100-ton gun batteries designed for the defence of the Grand Harbour. Construction works began in 1879 and were completed in 1886. It was armed with a single 100-ton Armstrong gun. The battery was basically pentagonal in plan, with its salient angle pointing out to sea. Its main defensive features were an enveloping ditch, three flanking caponiers, and a counterscarp gallery. The central element in the design of Rinella Battery was the gun emplacement with its underground magazines. The 100-ton gun was mounted en barbette on a traversing carriage, weighing some 45 tons, and fired over an eight-foot concrete parapet. The platform could be traversed through 180 degrees. Elevation was achieved by means of two hydraulic jacks below the barrel. The 100-ton gun was the only piece in service with the British Army which could not be man handled but had to be operated entirely by hydraulic power. The required pressure was built up by a steam engine and stored in an accumulator, all the apparatus being located in the vaulted casemates adjoining the gun emplacement.

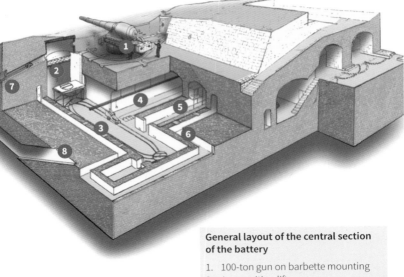

General layout of the central section of the battery

1. 100-ton gun on barbette mounting
2. Ammunition lift
3. Ammunition passage with narrow gauge rails for trolleys
4. Shell store
5. Cartridge store
6. Lighting passage
7. Loading ram
8. Passage leading down to caponiers

Aerial view of Rinella Battery showing its seaward-facing front with its concrete apron and caponiers in the ditch.

Top: The 100-ton RML gun as seen from the rear showing the main entrance and casemated gorge.
Above: The 100-ton RML gun.
Above right: Musketry loopholes of the counterscarp flanking gallery reached by an underground communication passage.
Right: View of one of the two loading chambers inside the battery.
Below: 100-ton gun.

GARDEN BATTERY
TAS-SLIEMA
Map 3 – L9
1889–1894

Garden Battery was completed on 14 December 1894 and consisted of a long and narrow work linked to the ditches of Fort Tigné and Cambridge Battery. The battery was protected on its seafront and rear by narrow ditches with no provision for enfilading fire. Internally, the enclosure was taken up by the concrete gun emplacements and their adjoining underground magazines and gun crew for one centrally-mounted 9.2-inch gun and two 6-inch guns. In 1906 there was a proposal for the armament of Garden Battery to be changed to two 9.2-inch Mk X BL guns but this was soon dropped as the battery was considered superfluous, and the work was eventually dismantled when a new battery was built at Tigné Point.

DELLE GRAZIE BATTERY
ĦAŻ-ŻABBAR
Map 3 – N11
1889–1893

The construction of Delle Grazie Battery was commenced in 1889 and the work was designed to take an armament of two 10-inch and two 6-inch BL guns. The battery was given a basic rectangular plan and was enveloped by a narrow ditch with vertical scarp and sloping counterscarp walls. Flanking defences were provided by two projecting bulbous caponiers and a defensible causeway containing the main entrance. The battery was completed in March 1893 at a cost of £16,344 but was soon to disappear from the list of those forts and batteries chosen to mount approved armament. By the outbreak of the First World War, its guns had already been dismantled and its role was eventually changed to that of an emplacement for a sound locator.

Wardija Battery is one of the very few works of fortification erected during WWI. It is an open work consisting of two emplacements for 6-inch BL guns and a battery command post. It was established as an examination battery but its role was taken over by Fort Campbell.

Wolseley Battery was built in 1897/1899 on the pattern of the Twydall profile, an experimental project at Twydall, near Chatham, in which low-profile earthwork defences replaced the permanent ditch and rampart defences of a few decades earlier. In plan, Wolseley battery was roughly oval and housed four barbette emplacements for 6-inch QF guns. The glacis in front of the gun emplacements sloped outwards and downwards at a gentle gradient terminating in a shallow scooped out ditch filled in with barbed wire entanglements. This embraced the whole curved front while the open gorge of the work, clearly visible and easily commanded from Fort Tas-Silġ to its rear, was secured by a nine-foot high iron palisade. Inside the enclosure, the only free-standing building was the guardhouse, which doubled as a caretaker's quarters.

The battery was retained in active use until 1906, when it was considered obsolete. Its guns were removed in 1916, when two of these were transferred to the Examination Battery at Wardija.

ŻONQOR BATTERY

MARSASKALA

Map 3 – N12
1882

Żonqor Battery was designed in the mid-1880s to defend Marsaskala Bay with three 7-inch guns. The pentagonal work, with its salient

angle facing southwards towards the bay, was surrounded by a ditch but lacked any caponiers or any other form of flanking defences. Internally, the enclosure was occupied by the three gun emplacements, a traverse, and underground storage rooms.

ST PAUL BATTERY

DELIMARA

Map 3 – N14
1881–1886

St Paul Battery, proposed in 1881, was to be armed with three 64-pdr RML guns on C pivot emplacements mounted on wrought-iron traversing platforms. In 1882, while it was still under construction, the armament was modified to three 7-inch of 6.5-ton RML guns mounted on six-foot parapet platforms. In plan, the battery was shaped like a capital D, with the curved part forming the main battery front facing seawards. The work was surrounded, around three-fourths of the enceinte, by a deep ditch devoid of any caponiers or any other form of flanking defences, while the land front was protected by a shallow fosse and a steel palisade. Internally, the

enclosure was occupied by the three gun emplacements cut into the thick parapet and a central large traverse that housed the shell and cartridge serving room beneath which were underground magazines. The work had no provision for gun crew accommodation, the garrison being stationed at the nearby Fort Tas-Silġ.

PEMBROKE BATTERY

PEMBROKE

Map 3 – J8
1897–1899

By the end of the nineteenth century the role of Fort Pembroke as a defensive coastal position was diminishing in importance. Its rifled muzzle-loading guns were by then considered obsolete, and it was proposed to replace them with two 9.2-inch BL guns. However, it was found to be much better to have the guns mounted outside the fort in a newly prepared position which would be less conspicuous from the sea than inside the old work itself. The new battery was first proposed in 1897 and the work was completed in less than two years. It was armed with two 9.2-inch BL Mk X guns (wire guns) mounted en barbette on pedestal barbette mountings. In plan, Pembroke Battery had a roughly oval form and was surrounded by a broad but relatively shallow revetted ditch. There were no provisions for flanking defence nor any infantry parapet to enable the small garrison to defend itself against a raid by a landing party. The battery was open at the gorge, enabling the garrison of Fort Pembroke to its rear to fire directly into the work. The only form of immediate defence was provided by a broad band of barbed wire entanglement. Only half of the battery, with one emplacement, survives.

1. Concrete emplacement for 9.2-inch Mk X BL guns (x2), mounted en barbette
2. Underground shell (x3) and cartridge store (x2)
3. Artillery store
4. B.C. Post with telephone room
5. Ordnance workshops
6. Perimeter barbed wire entanglement

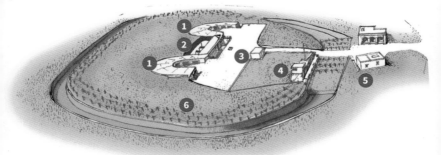

GĦARGĦUR HIGH-ANGLE BATTERY

ĦAL GĦARGĦUR

Map 3 – H8

1899

Gharghur High-Angle Battery was a work erected in 1899–1900 to mount six 10-inch RML guns mounted on special high-angle carriages. The battery was an open work, lacking any permanent or earthen fortifications. There were no blockhouses or infantry parapets to provide any defensible positions. The battery was nonetheless equipped with a number of buildings which served as barrack rooms, artillery stores, caretaker's quarters, and a battery command post.

TARĠA BATTERY

NAXXAR

Map 3 – F9

1887

Tarġa Battery was originally intended to defend the escarpment of the Victoria Lines west of Fort Mosta and was to be armed with four 64-pdr RML guns. The guns, however, were never installed for by 1888 it was no longer considered useful for the defence of the position.

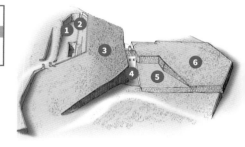

1. Internal courtyard with ramp leading down to main entrance
2. Stepped infantry banquette
3. Earthen slope of parapet
4. Caponier connecting battery to main body of the Victoria Lines
5. Masonry revetment
6. Earthen slope forming body of main battery (uncompleted)

FIELD DEFENCES

With the abandonment of the Victoria Lines as a front line of defence around 1903, the British military began to adopt a string of forward defensive positions intended to command the high ground and approaches from the various landing places and bays. By 1904 the British military began establishing ridge defences on the crests of various hills in the north of the island. By 1907 ridge defences had been established at Għajn Tuffieħa, St Paul's Bay, and Mellieħa.

These defences were little more than infantry trenches hewn in the rock along the crests of various ridges and hills. The earlier ones were topped by rubble walls fitted with loopholes for rifles, while later ones were equipped with machine-gun tables and underground bunkers.

The 1911 survey sheets also reveal some 16 field emplacements for howitzers and field guns spread around the island.

Top: Diagram showing a typical section to the trenches cut into the bedrock along the ridges.
Above and below: Parapet wall of the ridge defences at Mellieħa. (Map 3 – C6)

PILLBOXES

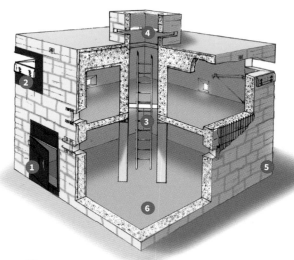

The concrete pillboxes and beachposts represent the last chapter in the development of fortifications and military architecture in Malta. Although never tested in battle, the small defensive works armed with machine guns and small anti-tank guns would have had to shoulder the brunt of the defence of Malta had the island been invaded by the Axis powers.

Hundreds of pillboxes were built immediately prior to the outbreak of the war in 1939 and in the opening years of the conflict. They were arranged and positioned tactically in a series of stop lines, being at the shore and retreating inland along ridges and valleys to create a succession of obstacles designed to delay an enemy's inland advance.

Although pillboxes were built in various shapes and sizes, one can distinguish three major categories. The earliest, built soon after the Abyssinian crisis, were low-lying structures, well camouflaged with a cladding of rubble stone. Those built around 1940 onwards were

1. Entrance hatch
2. Machine gun porthole
3. Metal ladder
4. Observation cupola
5. Steel reinforcement mesh
6. Ground floor

built more hurriedly to rectangular and box-like shapes where camouflage was applied in the form of painting.

Top and below: Cutaway diagrams showing two common typologies of concrete WWII pillboxes.

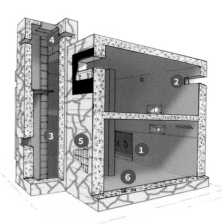

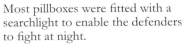

Most pillboxes were fitted with a searchlight to enable the defenders to fight at night.

The following pages provide various examples of the types of pillboxes which can be seen around the Maltese islands. None were built in Gozo.

Unfortunately, many pillboxes have disappeared since 1945, either because they were unceremoniously swept away to make room for modern development or simply because they were abandoned and left to decay and fall apart.

Being, more often than not, simple and plain structures of concrete, crudely built, they have tended to elicit little popular aesthetic response. With time, however, many of the surviving structures have blended into the countryside and earned their own place in the rural and coastal landscapes of the Maltese islands.

Top left: Concrete beachpost at Delimara. (Map 3 – N14)
Top right: Pillbox at Manikata. (Map 3 – C7)
Above: Pillbox at Għajn Tuta, Mellieħa. (Map 3 – B4)
Below: Concrete beachpost on the shoreline near Fort Ricasoli. (Map 3 – M10)

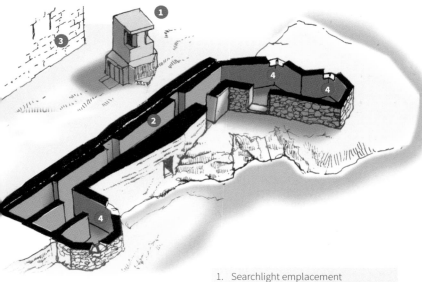

1. Searchlight emplacement
2. Communication passage
3. Westreme coastal battery
4. Machine gun emplacement

Above: Beach post (MB3) at Mellieħa Bay. (Map 3 – C5)
Below: The same beach post at Mellieħa Bay. The blockhouse of the seventeenth-century Westreme coastal battery in the background was also converted to form part of the beach defences.

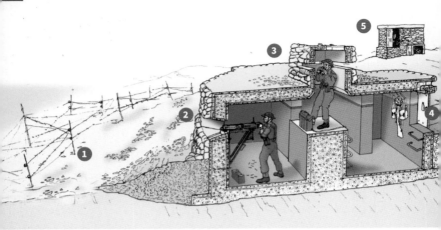

General layout of a typical 1938/1939 beachpost showing the main elements

1. Barbed wire entanglement placed in front of pillbox to protect against direct assault
2. Forward-facing machine gun embrasure
3. Commander's observation cupola
4. Entrance hatch
5. Detached searchlight emplacement

Left: Beachpost at Mġiebaħ Bay. (Map 3 – D5)
Below: Beachpost at Wied iż-Żurrieq. (Map 3 –

Above: Reserve Post R15, situated along the road at T'Alla u Ommu, in the limits of Naxxar. (Map 3 – G8)

Below: A camouflaged concrete pillbox facing Allied warships and landing barges outside Xgħajra (Ħaż-Żabbar) in July 1943. (Map 3 – M10)

Pillboxes and beachposts

1. Armier, l/o Mellieħa (Map 3 – C4)
2. Xgħajra (Map 3 – M10)
3. Birżebbuġa (Map 3 – L14)
4. Qawra (Map 3 – G6)
5. Selmun (Map 3 – E5)
6. Birżebbuġa (Map 3 – L14)
7. Marsaskala (Map 3 – O13)

Above left: Pillbox situated on the road from Naxxar to Salina. (Map 3 – G7)
Above right: Concrete pillbox at Selmun, l/o Mellieħa. (Map 3 – D5)
Below: Variant types of single-storey concrete pillboxes found in the northern parts of Malta.

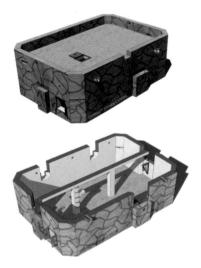
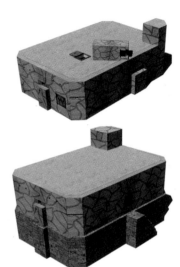

Below: Observation posts mimicking rustic buildings at Tal-Qroqq, near Mater Dei Hospital **(left)** (Map 3 – J10) **and San Ġwann, opposite San Ġwann Local Council (right).** (Map 3 – I9)

ANTI-AIRCRAFT BATTERIES

During the Second World War an important component of the island's defences were its anti-aircraft guns. These were mounted in batteries and protected by emplacements designed to shield the guns and their gunners from exploding bombs and machine-gun fire.

Many of the heavy anti-aircraft guns were mounted in prepared positions consisting of low concrete blast walls of rectangular or octagonal plan. Four gun emplacements, each fitted with ammunition storage areas and gun crew shelters, together with a command post and protected positions for height and range finders, made up a troop or battery of anti-aircraft guns.

The heavy anti-aircaft batteries were deployed roughly in three concentric circles, with the inner ring enveloping the harbour area and the other two the aerodromes and military installations respectively. The anti-aircraft batteries were grouped in two brigades. The heavy batteries were equipped with 4.5-inch guns and

The command post of an HAA battery with height- and range-finding instruments.

General layout of a 4.5-inch HAA gun emplacement

1. Concrete blast wall
2. Gun mounting holdfast
3. Ammunition hold
4. Partly underground gun crew shelters
5. Entrance to shelter

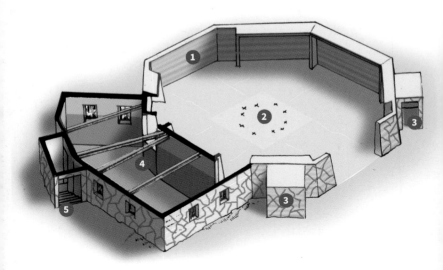

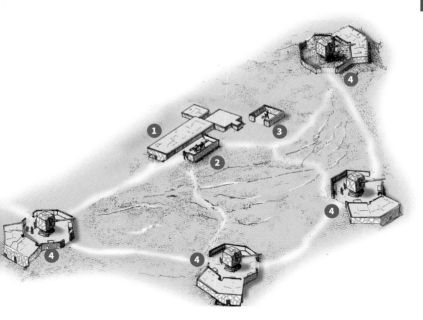

3.7-inch guns. Guns of smaller calibre, such as the 40-mm Bofors, were deployed around airfields and military installations and were meant to tackle the low-flying aircraft. These were usually protected by sangars, protective enclosures, and blast walls built with sandbags filled with earth or sand.

General layout of a typical heavy anti-aircraft (HAA) battery (troop) of 4.5-inch guns in protective turrets

1. Command post and shelter
2. Emplacement for height- and range-finding instruments
3. Emplacement for predictor
4. Concrete gun emplacements with blast walls and partly underground gun crew shelters

4.5-inch HAA gun in its turret and concrete gun emplacement with blast walls and gun crew accommodation. Note the camouflage netting.

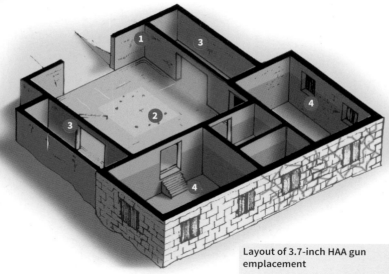

Layout of 3.7-inch HAA gun emplacement

1. Concrete blast wall
2. Gun-mounting holdfast
3. Ammunition hold
4. Partly underground gun crew shelter built of stone and roofed in concrete

Above: Aerial view of St Peter's HAA Battery situated close to St Rocco and Smart City. (Map 3 – M11)
Below: Concrete HAA emplacements on St Clements Bastion, Cottonera enceinte. (Map 3 – L11)

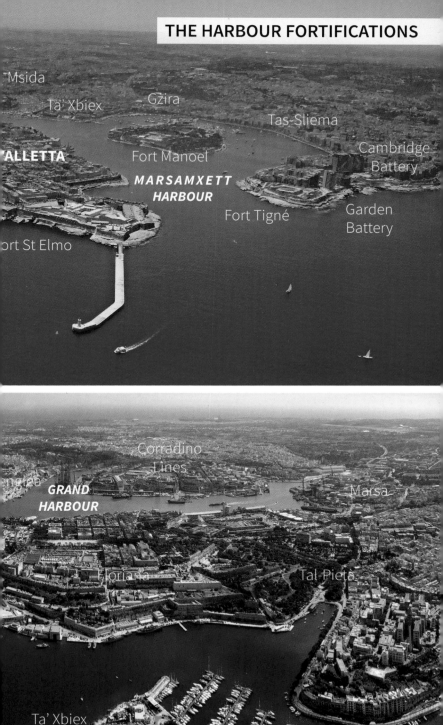

THE HARBOUR FORTIFICATIONS

Msida

Ta' Xbiex

Gzira

Tas-Sliema

VALLETTA

Fort Manoel

Cambridge Battery

MARSAMXETT HARBOUR

Fort Tigné

Garden Battery

Fort St Elmo

Corradino Lines

anglea

GRAND HARBOUR

Marsa

Floriana

Tal-Pietà

Ta' Xbiex

GLOSSARY

Advanced Work: Any work of fortification located outside the glacis yet within musketry range of the main enceinte.

Ashlar: Regular squared masonry used in the construction of walls and other structures.

Bailey: The open area or courtyard within a medieval castle.

Banquette: A continuous step or ledge at the base of a parapet, on which defenders would stand to fire their muskets over the top of the wall.

Barbette: A platform on which guns would be mounted to fire over a parapet. Guns mounted in such a manner are said to be mounted en barbette.

Barbican: An outer work defending the gate of a castle or citadel, frequently a fortified gatehouse.

Barrack: A building, sometimes fortified, designed to house the garrison of a fort.

Bassoforte: A low-level platform forming part of a faussebraye.

Bastion: A projection in the enceinte, comprised of two faces and two flanks, which would enable the garrison to defend the perimeter of a fort.

Batter: The inward inclination of the face of a wall from the vertical, receding as it rises.

Battery: A platform, usually protected by a parapet, built to mount cannon and mortars. **Coastal Battery**: A work for cannon, sometimes fortified against direct assault, designed to engage enemy ships close to the shore.

Battlement: A fortified parapet with merlons and crenels, or embrasures.

BL guns: Breach-loading guns.

Braye or Braga: A continuous outer work protecting the main enceinte of a fort, placed inside the main ditch and separated from both the scarp and counterscarp walls.

Breastwork: A wall, chest high, from behind which soldiers could fire their weapons.

Buttress: A mass of masonry built against a wall to reinforce it.

Capital of the Bastion: An imaginary line dividing the bastion in two, drawn through the point of the bastion.

Caponier (of communication): A sheltered, defensible passage across the ditch of a fort or cut through the glacis, linking the outworks to the main enceinte, sometimes used to provide additional flanking fire along the ditch.

Casemate: A vaulted chamber built into the thickness of the ramparts and used as a barrack or gun position (firing through embrasures).

Castle: A feudal stronghold, serving also as the fortified residence of a prince or lord.

Cavalier: A raised work where artillery would be placed to command the surrounding defences and the terrain outside a fort.

Citadel: A fortress or castle built to dominate or protect a town.

Coastal Battery: See **Battery**.

Coastal Redoubt: See **Redoubt**.

Corbel: A small projecting stone designed to support a beam or other horizontal member such as a balcony or machicolation.

Cordon: A rounded stone moulding or string course usually going all round the fort, most commonly found below the parapet.

Counterfort: A masonry buttress designed to reinforce the inner wall of a rampart.

Counterguard: A large outer work, open at the gorge and designed to protect the faces of bastions and ravelins.

Countermine Gallery: An underground tunnel excavated by defenders for the purpose of intercepting the enemy mines and siege works.

Counterscarp: The exterior side of the ditch facing the ramparts.

Counterscarp Gallery: A casemate within the counterscarp fitted with musketry loopholes to defend the ditch and scarp wall.

Couvre Porte: A small defensive work designed to cover the immediate approaches to the main entrance of a fortress.

Covertway or Covered Way: A path on top of the counterscarp, protected by a parapet formed from the crest of the glacis and designed to allow the defenders to access all the exterior parts of a fortress.

Crenellation: The openings in a parapet of a castle.

Curtain: The main wall of a fortification that links two adjacent towers or bastions.

Cyclopean Masonry: Large unworked boulders used to construct Bronze Age period fortification walls.

Demi-bastion: A half-bastion with one face, a flank, and a wing.

Demi-Lune: A small detached outwork, similar to a ravelin but smaller, placed before a curtain.

Detached Work: A work of fortification placed beyond the range of musket fire from the main enceinte of a fort, yet assisting in its defence.

Ditch: A wide, deep trench cut around a defensive work. When filled with water, it is termed a 'wet ditch' or moat, otherwise it is often referred to as a 'dry ditch'.

Drawbridge: A retractable bridge spanning a ditch, provided with lowering, raising or retreating mechanisms used to isolate the gate of a castle or fortress.

Echaugette, Gardjola or Guerite: A stone sentry box, cantilevered and projecting from the shoulder or salient of a bastion, intended to shelter a sentinel on guard duty.

Embrasure: An opening in a wall or parapet through which cannon could fire. The sides, generally splayed outward, were termed 'cheeks' and the inner narrow part, the 'throat'.

En Barbette: See **Barbette**.

Enceinte: The main works of fortification – walls, ramparts, and parapets – forming the primary enclosure of a fort or fortress.

Enfilading Fire: Fire from the flank of a bastion along the faces of the adjacent works.

Escarpe: See **Scarp**.

Escarpment: A ridge, natural or man-made, of high ground used as a fortified position owing to its defensive qualities against direct assault.

Escutcheon: Stone shields carved with heraldic coat of arms, often used to decorate gates and walls of castles and forts.

Fausse-braye: An outer rampart added to the walls of a fortress but lower in height than the main enceinte and preceded by a ditch.

Fort: A fortified military establishment served by a garrison.

Fortress: A fortified city or town, or any other major defensive work.

Gardjola: See **Echaugette**.

Gate: A main entrance (Porta Reale) into a castle, fort or fortress.

Glacis: The sloping ground in front of a fortress spanning from the top of the parapet of the covertway down until it reaches the open country, cleared of all obstacles and vegetation in order to expose an advancing enemy to direct line of fire.

Gorge: The open rear part of a rampart, facing the inner works of a fort.

Guerite: See **Echaugette**.

Guthrie Rolling Bridge: A retractable drawbridge used in nineteenth-century British forts.

Howitzer: An artillery piece used to fire shells over a high trajectory.

Keep: The innermost part of a fortress, designed to act as a place of last resort.

Listening Gallery: A chamber at the end of a countermine tunnel used to detect the sounds of tools of enemy miners in the event of a siege.

Loophole: A small opening in a wall through which small arms used to be fired.

Lunette: A small ravelin, often placed along the covertway or on the glacis.

Machicoulis, Machicolation: An overhanging structure in the form of a balcony, supported on corbels with floor openings between them through which missiles and combustibles could be dropped on attackers below.

Magazine: A place for the storage of gunpowder, arms, provisions or goods.

Merlon: The solid part of a parapet between two embrasures or crenels.

Mine: An underground cavity or tunnel excavated by besiegers under a work of fortification for the purpose of destroying it with explosives or other combustibles.

Musketry Gallery: Part of a work of fortification designed to allow soldiers armed with muskets or rifles to fire their weapons from within the safety of a rampart.

Muzzle-loading Gun: A gun loaded from the front end of the barrel.

Observation Post: A room or position used to observe enemy movements (infantry, ships, etc.) or the fall of shot from artillery fire (in the case of a battery).

Orillion: A projecting shoulder of a bastion designed to cover the flank.

Parados: A large earthen/masonry traverse erected inside a fort to protect against artillery bombardment. Can contain casemates.

Parapet: A work of earth and/or masonry forming a protective wall over which defenders used to fire their weapons.

Pas-de-Souris: A staircase giving access from the ditch to the covertway and the place-of-arms.

Piazza Bassa: A low platform or casemated battery in the flank of a bastion.

Place-of-Arms: An area on the covertway used for troops to assemble.

Polverista: A magazine used for the safe storage of gunpowder and munitions.

Postern: See **Sally Port**.

QF Guns: Quick-firing guns.

Quoin: A hard stone used to reinforce a salient, corner or edge of wall.

Rampart: A thick wall of earth or masonry forming the main defence of a fortress, usually reinforced from the rear with counterforts and terreplein.

Ravelin: A triangular shaped outwork placed in front of a curtain to shield it from bombardment.

Redan: A triangular work placed in advance of a main work. In coastal batteries, the redan is fitted with loopholes and connected to the blockhouse/s.

Redan Trace: A system of fortification consisting of a series of redans forming a serrated edge.

Redoubt: A small fortified work designed as an infantry stronghold, sometimes built inside a bastion or ravelin as a retrenchment, or in the field as a defence against cavalry attack. **Coastal Redoubt**: An infantry stronghold placed on the shoreline against a seaborne invasion.

Reserve Post: A fall-back defensive position or fortification.

Revetment: A retaining wall of a rampart.

RML Guns: Rifled muzzle-loading guns.

Salient: An angular work which projects outward from the interior.

Salient Angle: An angle pointing outward.

Sally Port or Postern: A concealed gate or underground passage leading from inside the fortress into the ditch; a postern.

Sangar: An improvised protective enclosure built with sandbags.

Scarp or Escarp: The wall of a fortified work which forms the side of the ditch facing outwards towards the counterscarp.

Shoulder of a Bastion: The corner formed by the intersection of the face and flank of a bastion.

Siege: An organized, systematic attack on a fort or fortress.

Sortie: A sudden counter-attack on the besiegers by the garrison of a defensive work.

Spur: An arrow-shaped work.

Spur of a Bastion: Sharp-edged buttress placed at the foot of a rounded salient of a bastion.

Tenaille: A work constructed in a main ditch between bastions, in front of a curtain, erected to protect the curtain from the battering of enemy cannon fire.

Terreplein: Packing of earth forming the body of a rampart.

Trace: The perimeter or ground plan of a fortified work.

Traverse: A defensive barrier consisting of a parapet or simple wall placed at right angles to the main line of defence, in order to protect the defenders from flanking fire.

Turret: A small and slender tower projecting from the main rampart.

Vents: Vertical ventilation shafts or openings intended to allow smoke to escape from inside casemates and batteries.

The Fortress Builders – Fortifications Interpretation Centre (FIC), St Mark Street, Valletta

The FIC is an information centre run by the Restoration Directorate and is designed to introduce visitors to the history and development of military architecture in the Maltese islands.

T: +356 21228594
E: fic.mti@gov.mt

St Agatha Tower, Mellieħa

This 17th-century coastal tower run by Din l-Art Ħelwa (NGO) contains a small exhibition about coastal fortifications and offers excellent panoramic views of the channel between Malta and Gozo from its rooftop.

T: +356 21225952
W: info@dinlarthelwa.org

Fort St Elmo – National War Museum, Valletta

This important fort run by Heritage Malta houses the National War Museum and is dedicated to the various periods of Maltese history. It contains exhibitions highlighting Malta's important role in various conflicts including WWI and WWII.

T: +356 21233088
W: www.heritagemalta.org

Wignacourt Tower, St Paul's Bay

Commanding a strategic promontory just off the Buġibba promenade, this early 17th-century coastal tower run by Din l-Art Ħelwa (NGO) contains a small exhibition with scale models of the fortifications.

T: +356 21225952
W: info@dinlarthelwa.org

Fort St Angelo, Birgu

This historic harbour fort managed by Heritage Malta contains various exhibitions related to the history of the fort and dramatic panoramic views of the Grand Harbour.

Tel: +356 25401800
W: www.heritagemalta.org

Fort Rinella, Kalkara

This 19th-century British work of coastal fortification, run by Fondazzjoni Wirt Artna (NGO), is located near Fort Ricasoli and provides a unique opportunity to see the 100-ton gun up close, together with various exhibits related to British garrison life.

T: +356 21800992
E: info@wirtartna.org